Four t h

THE WASHINGTON NOTARY LAW PRIMER

All the hard-to-find information every Washington Notary Public needs to know!

National Notary Association

Published by:

National Notary Association
9350 De Soto Ave., P.O. Box 2402
Chatsworth, CA 91313-2402
Telephone: 1-818-739-4000
FAX: 1-818-700-0920
E-mail: nna@nationalnotary.org
Web site: www.nationalnotary.org

Copyright © 1999 National Notary Association
ALL RIGHTS RESERVED. No part of this book may be reproduced in any form without permission in writing from the publisher.

This information is provided to aid comprehension of state Notary Public requirements and should not be construed as legal advice. Please consult an attorney for inquiries relating to legal matters.

Fourth Edition
First Edition © 1986

ISSN No. 1098-6510
ISBN No. 1-891133-17-9

Table of Contents

Introduction 1

How to Become a Washington Notary Public 3

Tools of the Trade 6

10 Most-Asked Questions 8

Steps to Proper Notarization 13

Notary Laws Explained 18
    The Notary Commission 18
    Official Notarial Acts 22
    Practices and Procedures 38
    Misconduct, Fines and Penalties 62

Test Your Knowledge 68

Washington Laws Pertaining to Notaries Public 74

Office of the Washington Department of Licensing 105

Bureaus of Vital Statistics 106

Hague Convention Nations 111

About the Publisher 114

Index 115

Introduction

You are to be commended on your interest in Washington Notary law! Purchasing *The Washington Notary Law Primer* identifies you as a conscientious professional who takes your official responsibilities seriously.

In few fields is the expression "more to it than meets the eye" truer than in Notary law. What often appears on the surface to be a simple procedure may, in fact, have important legal considerations.

The purpose of *The Washington Notary Law Primer* is to provide you with a resource to help decipher the many intricate laws that affect notarization. In doing so, the *Primer* will acquaint you with all important aspects of Washington Notary law and with prudent notarial practices in general.

This 1998 *Primer* has been updated to include all recent pertinent law changes.

While *The Washington Notary Law Primer* begins with informative chapters on how to obtain your appointment, what tools the Notary needs, often-asked questions, and critical steps in notarization, the heart of this book is the chapter entitled "Notary Laws Explained." Here, we take you through the myriad of Notary laws and put them in easy-to-understand terms. Every pertinent section of the law is analyzed and explained, as well as topics not covered by Washington law but nonetheless of vital concern to you as a Notary.

For handy reference, we have reprinted the complete text of the statutes of Washington that relate to the duties of Notaries Public. In addition, we have included the addresses and telephone numbers of the Washington Department of Licensing office and Bureaus of Vital Statistics, plus a list of nations that

WASHINGTON NOTARY LAW PRIMER

are parties to the Hague Convention, a treaty which simplifies the process of authentication.

Whether you're about to be appointed for the first time, or a longtime Notary, we're sure *The Washington Notary Law Primer* will provide you with new insights and understanding. Your improved comprehension of Washington Notary law will naturally result in greater competence as a professional Notary Public.

                        Milton G. Valera
                        President
                        National Notary Association

How to Become a Washington Notary Public

1. Ensure that you comply with the basic qualifications for a Washington Notary appointment.

First, you must be a legal resident of the state or a resident of an adjoining state who works or conducts business in Washington. Second, you must be 18 years of age or older. Third, you must not have been convicted of a serious crime. Fourth, you must not have had any previous Notary appointment or professional license revoked in Washington or any other state. And fifth, you must be able to read and write the English language.

U.S. citizenship is not required as long as you legally reside in this country under federal law. There is no minimum time of state residency — you can apply for an appointment on the same day you enter Washington.

2. Obtain an appointment application form.

The official application and information packet for a Washington Notary appointment is available from the Department of Licensing by calling 1-360-753-3836. You may also obtain an application in person or through the mail from: Department of Licensing, Business & Occupations Unit, Notaries Public Licensing Program, P.O. Box 9027, Olympia, WA 98507-9027.

The application and other information is also available via the Internet at *www.wa.gov/dol/bpd/notfront.htm*. From this site, you can request an application via e-mail or download the form directly onto your computer.

If you are renewing your Notary appointment, you must follow the same procedures as if applying for the first time. However, when applying for reappointment, you need not have your application endorsed if you are applying for renewal before expiration of your current commission.

3. Complete the application form.

Read the entire application packet and complete all questions, typing or printing neatly in ink. Be aware that any misstatement or omission of information may be cause for denial or later revocation of a Notary appointment.

You must have your application endorsed by three people who are at least 18 years old, unrelated to you and eligible to vote in Washington.

4. Take your oath.

The Notary application will have a personal declaration containing an oath of office. Go to a Notary Public, sign your appointment application in his or her presence and take your oath. Be sure to sign your name exactly as it is to appear on your Certificate of Appointment.

5. Obtain your bond.

A $10,000 bond is required for Washington Notaries. Contact an insurance company authorized to write surety bonds in Washington. The bond must cover your entire four-year Notary term. All spaces on the bond must be completed, and the name and signature on the bond must be identical to the name and signature on the application.

6. Submit the application with the appropriate fee and your Notary bond.

The completed and signed application and bond and a $20 fee payable to "Washington State Treasurer" must be mailed or delivered to the Department of Licensing, Business & Occupations Unit at the address on page 3.

"Renewing" Notaries will receive a new appointment number and expiration date, and will be required to obtain a new seal or stamp. The new seal or stamp may not be used until the effective date on the new Certificate of Appointment.

7. Obtain an official Notary seal or stamp.

Once your application has been approved, the Division of Licensing will send you your official Notary Certificate of Appointment. Send a copy of the Certificate to a company of your choice to purchase a Notary seal or stamp. See "Notary Seal or Stamp" on pages 49–51 for the specific requirements of Washington law regarding a Notary seal or stamp.

Once you have purchased your seal or stamp and journal, and reached the effective date specified on your Certificate of Appointment, you are ready to notarize. ∎

Tools of the Trade

There are several tools that Notaries need to carry out their duties lawfully and efficiently. These tools are as important to the Notary as a hammer and saw are to the carpenter.

Inking Stamp

The inked rubber stamp affixes a photographically reproducible impression in indelible ink. It is a convenient official seal for notarizing documents that will be submitted to a public recorder for microfilming. The Washington Notary's stamp must meet numerous specific standards. (See "Notary Seal or Stamp," pages 49–51.)

Seal Embosser

The embosser may be used by itself as an official Washington Notary seal; however, when an embosser is affixed on documents that will be publicly recorded and microfilmed (deeds, etc.), the resulting impression *must* be smudged with ink, graphite or carbon to become photographically reproducible. However, when used in conjunction with an inking stamp, the embossment does not have to be smudged. Many Notaries use an embosser as a fraud deterrent — embossing pages and certificates together — in addition to an inking stamp. Because photocopies of documents can easily pass as originals, the embossment can be used to distinguish an original from a photocopy.

Journal of Notarial Acts

Though Washington law does not require Notaries to keep a record of their official acts, the National Notary Association encourages such recordkeeping by every Notary.

TOOLS OF THE TRADE

The Notary's journal provides a record of notarial transactions that may be used as evidence in court proceedings and is the best protection for a Notary against claims of misconduct or negligence.

Bound Notary journals with numbered pages have proven to be the safest and most fraud-resistant type of record book. By contrast, loose-leaf books are the least secure. (See "Journal of Notarial Acts and Notarial Records, pages 41–43.)

Jurat Stamp

The jurat stamp impresses the jurat wording "Subscribed and sworn to before me this _____ day of _____ (month), _____ (year) by _____." The jurat stamp is more convenient (and safer, since critical wording will not be omitted) than typing the wording on each affidavit that requires it.

Venue Stamp

The venue stamp is used in conjunction with the jurat stamp in a jurat. The phrase, "State of _____, County of _____," indicates where the jurat was executed. Also usable for acknowledgments.

Fingerprinting Device

Though not required by law, asking a signer to leave a thumbprint in the Notary's journal is a strong deterrent to forgers. Small, inexpensive devices make taking a print easy.

Notarial Certificates

Preprinted notarial certificates for acknowledgments, jurats and copy certification by document custodian are available.

Errors and Omissions Insurance

Notary errors and omissions insurance provides protection for Notaries who are sued for damages resulting from unintentional notarial mistakes. In the event of a lawsuit, the "E&O" insurance company will provide and pay for the Notary's legal counsel and absorb any damages levied by a court or agreed to in a settlement, up to the policy coverage limit. Errors and omissions insurance does not cover the Notary for intentional misconduct. ■

As a full-service organization, the National Notary Association makes available to Washington Notaries all notarial items required by law, custom and convenience.

10 Most-Asked Questions

Every Notary has a question or two about whether and how to notarize. But there are certain questions that pop up again and again. These top 10 are asked repeatedly at the National Notary Association's seminars, its annual National Conference of Notaries Public and through its *Notary Information Service*.

As with most questions about notarization, the answer to these 10 is not always a simple "yes" or "no." Rather, the answer is, "It depends...."

Here's what every Notary wants to know:

1. Can I notarize a will?

Sometimes. A Notary should only notarize a document described as a will if clear instructions and a notarial certificate are provided. If the signer of the will is relying on the Notary for advice on how to proceed, the Notary should tell the individual to see an attorney.

Laws regarding wills differ from state to state. Some states do not require notarization of wills, while others allow it as one of several witnessing options. Often it is not the will itself that is notarized, but accompanying affidavits signed by witnesses.

The danger in notarizing wills is that would-be testators who have drafted their own wills without legal advice may believe that notarization will make their wills legal and valid. However, even when notarized, such homemade wills may be worthless because the testators failed to obtain the proper number of witnesses or omitted important information.

In fact, notarization itself may actually void an otherwise properly executed handwritten (holographic) will, because courts have occasionally held that any writing on the document other than the testator's invalidates the will.

2. Can I notarize for a stranger with no identification?

Yes. If identification of a signer cannot be based on personal knowledge or identification documents (ID cards), a Notary may rely on the oath or affirmation of one personally known credible identifying witness to identify an unknown signer.

The Notary should personally know the credible identifying witness, who must personally know the document signer. This establishes a chain of personal knowledge from the Notary to the credible identifying witness to the signer.

A credible identifying witness should be someone the Notary believes to be trustworthy and impartial. If a person has a financial or other beneficial interest in a document, that individual could not be a reliable witness.

When no credible identifying witness is available to identify a stranger without IDs, the Notary may have no choice but to tell the signer to find a personally known Notary or a friend who personally knows a Notary, if the signer is unable to obtain an adequate identification document.

3. Can I notarize a photograph?

No. To simply stamp and sign a photograph is improper. A Notary's signature and seal must appear only on a notarial certificate (such as an acknowledgment or jurat) accompanying a written statement signed by another person.

However, a signature on a written statement referring to an accompanying or attached photograph may be notarized; if the photograph is large enough, the statement and notarial certificate might even appear on its reverse side. Such a format may be acceptable when notarized photos are requested by persons seeking medical or health licenses, or by legal resident aliens renewing foreign passports.

A word of caution here: a Notary should always be suspicious about notarizing a photo-bearing card or document that could be fraudulently used as a supposed "official" ID.

4. What if there's no room for my seal or if it smears?

Usually, if notarial wording printed on a document leaves no room for a seal, a loose certificate can be attached and filled out instead, if the certificate wording is substantially the same as on the document.

If an initial seal impression is unreadable and there is ample room on the document, another impression can be affixed nearby. The illegibility of the first impression will indicate why a second seal impression was necessary. The Notary should record in the journal that a second seal was applied.

A Notary should *never* attempt to fix an imperfect seal impression with pen, ink or correction fluid. This may be viewed as evidence of tampering and cause the document's rejection by a recorder.

5. Can I notarize signatures on photocopies of documents?

Yes. A photocopy may be notarized as long as it bears an *original* signature. That is, the photocopy must have been signed with pen and ink. A photocopied signature may *never* be notarized.

Note that some public recorders will not accept notarized signatures on photocopied sheets because the document will not adequately reproduce in microfilming.

When carbon copies are made, the Notary will sometimes be asked to conform rather than to notarize the copies. To conform a copy, the Notary reaffixes the official seal or stamp on the copy (carbon will not readily transfer a seal or stamp impression) and writes "conformed copy" prominently across the copy.

6. May I notarize for customers only?

No. As a public official, a Notary is not appointed to serve just the customers or clients of any one business, even when the Notary's employer has paid for the bond, appointment fees and notarial supplies. There is no such officer as a "Notary Private."

It is ethically improper — although hardly ever explicitly prohibited by statute — to discriminate between customers and noncustomers in offering or refusing to offer notarial services and in charging or not charging fees.

Discrimination against anyone who presents a lawful request for notarization is not a suitable policy for a public official commissioned to serve all of the public equally. Also, such discrimination can provide the basis for lawsuits.

7. Can I notarize a document in a language I can't read?

Perhaps. As long as the notarial certificate and document signature are in a language the Notary *can* read, Washington Notaries are not expressly prohibited from notarizing a document written in a language they *cannot* read.

However, there are certain difficulties and dangers in doing so. The main difficulty for the Notary is making an accurate journal description of an unreadable document; the main danger is that the document may be blatantly fraudulent. It is always preferable to refer the signer of such documents to a bilingual Notary who can read the language.

Under no circumstances should a notarization be performed if the Notary and the principal signer cannot communicate in the same language.

8. Can I certify a copy of a birth certificate?

No. While Washington Notaries are authorized to certify copies, they are strongly discouraged from certifying copies of documents that are either public records or publicly recordable.

Only an officer in a bureau of vital statistics should certify a copy of a birth certificate or other vital public record; a Notary's "certification" of a birth or death record may actually lend credibility to a counterfeit or tampered document. Only a county recording official should certify a copy of a deed or other recordable instrument.

The types of documents that Washington Notaries may properly certify copies of are original personal papers such as college diplomas, letters and in-house business documents.

9. Does a document have to be signed in my presence?

No and yes. Documents requiring acknowledgments normally do not need to be signed in the Notary's presence. However, the signer *must* appear before the Notary at the time of notarization to acknowledge that he or she freely signed for the purposes stated in the document.

An acknowledgment certificate indicates that the signer personally appeared before the Notary, was identified by the Notary, and acknowledged to the Notary that the document was freely signed.

On the other hand, documents requiring a jurat *must* indeed be signed in the Notary's presence, as dictated by the typical jurat wording, "Subscribed (signed) and sworn to before me...."

In executing a jurat, a Notary guarantees that the signer personally appeared before the Notary, was given an oath or affirmation by the Notary, and signed in the Notary's presence. In addition, even though the jurat wording may not indicate that the Notary positively identified the signer, Washington law requires Notaries to do so.

10. Can I notarize for a family member?

Yes and no. Although state law does not directly prohibit notarizing for family members, the National Notary Association recommends that a Notary should not notarize in these cases. Notaries who do so may violate guidelines prohibiting a direct beneficial interest — especially in notarizing for spouses.

Besides the possibility of a financial interest in notarizing for a relative, there may be an "emotional interest" that can prevent the Notary from acting impartially. For example, a Notary who is asked to notarize a contract signed by his brother might attempt to persuade the sibling to sign or not sign. As a brother, the individual is entitled to exert influence — but this is entirely improper for a Notary.

Even if a Notary has no direct beneficial interest in the document and does not attempt to influence the signer, notarizing for a relative could subject the document to a legal challenge if other parties to the transaction allege that the Notary could not have acted impartially. ■

Steps to Proper Notarization

What constitutes reasonable care? If a Notary can convincingly show that he or she used every reasonable precaution expected of a person of ordinary prudence and intelligence, then the Notary has exercised reasonable care — a shield against liability.

While it would be impossible to compile an all-inclusive list of the actions constituting reasonable care in every possible case, the following 14-step checklist will help Notaries avoid the most common pitfalls.

1. Require every signer to personally appear.

The signer *must* appear in person before the Notary on the date and in the county stated in the notarial certificate. "Personal appearance" means the signer is in the Notary's physical presence — face to face in the same room. A telephone call is not acceptable in lieu of personal appearance.

2. Make a careful identification.

The Notary should identify every document signer through either personal knowledge, the oath of a credible identifying witness, or through reliable identification documents (ID cards). When using ID cards, the Notary must examine them closely to detect alteration, counterfeiting or evidence that they are issued to an impostor. Don't rely on a type of card with which you are unfamiliar, unless you check it against a reference such as the *U.S. Identification Manual* or the *ID Checking Guide*.

3. Feel certain the signer understands the transaction.

A conscientious and careful Notary will be certain not only of the signer's identity and willingness to sign, but also will make a layperson's judgment about the signer's ability to understand the document.

While Washington law does not expressly require the Notary to make a judgment about the signer's ability to understand the transaction, it is in the Notary's best interest to do so. A document signer who is not able to respond intelligibly in a simple conversation with the Notary should not be considered responsible to sign at that moment.

If in doubt, the Notary can ask the signer if he or she understands the document and can explain its purpose. Or, if the notarization is to be performed in a medical environment while the signer is under medical care, the signer's doctor can be consulted for a professional opinion.

4. Check the signature.

The Notary must make sure that the document signer signs the same name appearing on the identification presented.

To check for possible forgery, the Notary should compare the signature that the person leaves in the journal of notarial acts against the signatures on the document and on the IDs. Also, it should be noted whether the signer appears to be laboring on the journal signature, a possible indication of forgery in progress. In certain circumstances, it may be acceptable to make allowances for a signer who is signing with an abbreviated form of his name (John D. Smith instead of John David Smith), as long as the individual is signing with *less* than and not *more* than what is on the identification document.

5. Look for blank spaces.

Although not expressly prohibited by Washington law, notarization of incomplete documents is an unwise practice.

Documents with blank spaces have a great potential for fraudulent misuse. A borrower, for example, might sign an incomplete promissory note, trusting the lender to fill it out, and then later find that the lender has written in an amount in excess of what was actually borrowed.

If the blanks are inapplicable and intended to be left unfilled, the signer may be asked to line through each space (using ink), or to write in "not applicable" or "NA."

6. Scan the document.

Notaries are not required to read the documents they

notarize. However, they should note certain important particulars about a document, such as its title, for recording in the journal of notarial acts. Notaries must be sure to count and record the number of pages; this can show whether pages are later fraudulently added or removed.

7. Check the document's date.

For acknowledgments, the date of signing on the document must either precede or be the same as the date of the notarization; it should not follow it. For a jurat, the document signing date and the notarization date must be the same.

A document dated to follow the date on its notarial certificate risks rejection by a recorder, who may question how the document could have been notarized before it was signed.

8. Keep a journal of notarial acts.

While not required by Washington law, a journal record is a vital part of any notarial act. If a notarized document is lost or altered, or if certain facts about the transaction are later challenged, the Notary's journal becomes valuable evidence. It can protect the rights of all parties to a transaction and help Notaries defend themselves against false accusations.

The Notary should include *all* the pertinent details of the notarization in the journal, such as the date and type of notarization, the date and type of document, the name and address of the signer, how this person was identified and notarial fees charged, if any. In addition, any other pertinent data, such as the representative capacity the signer is claiming, may be entered. Signers may also be asked to leave a signature and/or a thumbprint in the Notary's journal as a deterrent to fraud, though this is not required by law in Washington.

9. Complete the journal entry first.

The Notary should complete the journal entry entirely *before* filling out the notarial certificate. This prevents a signer from leaving before the important record of the notarization is made in the journal.

10. Make sure the document has notarial wording.

If a notarial certificate does not come with the document, the Notary must ask the document signer what type of notarization — acknowledgment, jurat or other — is required. The Notary may then type the appropriate notarial wording on the document or attach a preprinted, loose certificate.

If the signer does not know what type of notarization is required, he or she should contact the document's issuing or receiving agency to determine the type of notarization needed. This decision is *rarely* the Notary's to make unless the Notary is also an attorney or an appropriately trained expert. (See "Selecting Certificates," page 46.)

11. Be attentive to details.

When filling out the certificate, the Notary needs to make sure the venue correctly identifies the place of notarization. If the venue is preprinted and incorrect, the Notary must line through the incorrect state and/or county, write in the proper site of the notarization, and initial and date the change.

Also, the Notary must pay attention to spaces on the notarial certificate that indicate the number and gender of the document signers, as well as how they were identified — for example, leave the plural "(s)" in "person(s)" untouched or cross it out, as appropriate.

12. Affix your signature and seal or stamp properly.

Notaries should sign *exactly* the same name appearing on their commissioning papers. And they must never forget to affix their official seals or stamps — a common reason for rejection of a document by a recorder. The seal or stamp should be placed as close to the Notary's signature as possible without overprinting it.

13. Attach 'loose' certificates correctly.

Recording laws in Washington require that "loose" Notary certificates be treated and attached like other document pages. Attached certificates should be the same size as the other pages in the document and provide a margin of at least one inch on all sides. A loose certificate page should immediately follow a document's signature page.

Notaries can protect against the removal of loose certificates by embossing them together with the documents and writing on them the particulars of the document to which the certificate is attached. For example, the notation, "This certificate is attached to a 15-page partnership agreement between John Smith and Mary Doe, signed July 14, 2001," would deter fraudulent removal and reattachment of a loose certificate.

14. Don't give advice.

Every state prohibits nonattorneys from practicing law. Notaries should *never* prepare or complete documents for others, nor give advice on any matter relating to a document unless they are attorneys or professionals certified or licensed in a relevant area of expertise. The nonattorney Notary should *never* choose the type of certificate or notarization a document needs, since this decision can have important legal ramifications. The Notary could be held liable for any damages resulting from an incorrectly chosen certificate or notarization. ■

Notary Laws Explained

In layperson's language, this chapter discusses and clarifies key parts of the laws of Washington that regulate Notaries Public. Most of these laws are reprinted in full in "Washington Laws Pertaining to Notaries Public," beginning on page 74.

Most provisions cited are from Chapter 42.44, "Notaries Public," of the Revised Code of Washington (RCW). Other notarial rules are cited from Chapter 308-30, "Notaries Public," of the Washington Administrative Code (WAC).

THE NOTARY COMMISSION

Application for Commission

Qualifications. To become a Notary in Washington, the applicant must: (RCW 42.44.020 and 42.44.030)

1) Be at least 18 years old;

2) Be a legal resident of Washington, or a resident of an adjoining state who is regularly employed or conducts business in Washington;

3) Be able to read and write the English language;

4) Not have had a Notary appointment or other professional license revoked in Washington or any other state; and

5) Not have been convicted of a felony or serious crime involving moral turpitude, misrepresentation, fraud or similar offense;

In addition, the applicant must properly complete and submit the Notary application, including the endorsements and personal declaration, and pay the required fees. (See "Personal Declaration," page 20.)

Endorsements Required. Each application must be endorsed by three state residents who are unrelated to the applicant, are 18 years of age or older and are eligible to vote in Washington. The endorsements are printed on the application form.

Endorsements are not required for persons applying for reappointment as long as the person submits the application for reappointment before the expiration of the current appointment. (RCW 42.44.070)

Application Fee. The total fee for a Notary appointment applicant is $20, payable to the "Washington State Treasurer." (WAC 308-30-100)

Rejection of Application. The Department of Licensing may deny a Notary application for reasons that include: (RCW 42.44.030)

- Failure to meet commission qualifications;

- A false statement knowingly made in the application;

- A conviction for a felony or a crime involving moral turpitude, misrepresentation, fraud or similar offense;

- Revocation, suspension or restriction of another professional license in Washington or any other state;

- Engaging in official misconduct, whether or not criminal penalties resulted; or

- Performing a notarial act with gross negligence.

Notary Bond

Required. Washington Notaries are required to obtain a $10,000 surety bond. (RCW 42.44.020)

Filing the Bond. The bond must be submitted with the Notary

Public application. (RCW 42.44.020)

Surety. The required Notary bond must be issued by a licensed bonding or insurance company. The dates on the bond must exactly coincide with the dates of the Notary's four-year term. (RCW 42.44.020)

Purpose. The Notary bond protects the public from a Notary's misconduct or negligence. The bond does not protect the Notary, who is personally liable for all damages resulting from illegal or improper performance of notarial duties.
The bond's surety company agrees to pay damages totalling up to the bond amount to persons who suffer financially because of the Notary's improper acts, intentional or not, in the event the Notary does not have the financial resources to pay these damages. The surety will seek compensation from the Notary for any damages it has to pay out on the Notary's behalf.

Liable for All Damages. A Notary and the surety company bonding the Notary may be sued by any person who has been damaged by the Notary's official acts. The surety is liable only up to the amount of the bond, but a Notary may be found liable for any amount of money.

Personal Declaration

Requirement. Each prospective Notary must take and sign the Notary application and personal declaration in the presence of a Notary Public or other person authorized to administer oaths in Washington. A Notary applicant cannot notarize his or her own personal declaration. (RCW 42.44.020)

Jurisdiction

Statewide. Notaries may perform official acts throughout the state of Washington but not beyond the state borders. A Notary may not witness a signing outside Washington and then return to the state to perform the notarization; all parts of a notarial act must be performed at the same time and place within the state of Washington. (RCW 42.44.060)

Term of Office

Four-Year Term. A Washington Notary Public's term of office is four years, beginning on the effective date specified on the

Certificate of Appointment and ending at midnight on the appointment expiration date. (RCW 42.44.060)

Resignation

Purpose. A person must officially resign the notarial appointment if: (RCW 42.44.020, 42.44.170 and WAC 308-30-150)

- The person no longer desires to be a Notary Public in Washington;

- The person no longer resides in or maintains a business or place of employment in Washington; or

- The person can no longer read or write English; or

- The person is found legally incompetent by judicial ruling.

Procedure. To resign, a Notary must submit written notice, and the stamp or seal, to the Department of Licensing. (RCW 42.44.170 and WAC 308-30-040)

If a notarial journal is maintained by the Notary, state officials direct the Notary to retain the journal for as long as the Notary is subject to potential legal action under the statute of limitations.

Change of Address

Notify Secretary of State. Whenever a Notary changes his or her address, the Notary must inform the Department of Licensing of the address change. The notice should include the Notary's name and appointment number, and the old and new addresses. There is no fee to file a change of address. (WAC 308-30-060)

Moving Out of State. If a Notary moves his or her residence — or, if a commuting nonresident, his or her place of employment — out of Washington, he or she vacates the office of Notary. Such a move requires the Notary to resign the appointment. (See "Resignation," above.) (RCW 42.44.020 and WAC 308-30-150)

Change of Name

Procedure. A Notary may change the name on his or her Notary Public appointment by notifying the Department of Licensing in writing. The notification must be accompanied by a bond rider from the Notary's bonding company and a $15 fee which provides for a duplicate Notary Certificate of Appointment showing the new name. (WAC 308-30-060 and 308-30-100)

New Seal Required. When a Notary files a name change with the Department of Licensing, he or she will receive a duplicate Notary Certificate showing the new name. The Notary must present a copy of the certificate to a qualified seal manufacturer in order to purchase a new seal and/or stamp. (WAC 308-30-010)

Exception. State officials allow Notaries who are nearing renewal (e.g., within a few months) to wait until they renew their commission to change their name on the application.

OFFICIAL NOTARIAL ACTS

Authorized Acts

Notaries may perform the following official acts: (RCW 42.44.010 and 42.44.080)

- Acknowledgments, certifying that a signer personally appeared before the Notary, was identified by the Notary, and acknowledged freely signing the document. (See pages 23–28.)

- Certified Copies, attesting that a photocopy of an original document is true and complete. (See pages 28–29.)

- Depositions, certifying that the spoken words of a witness were accurately taken down in writing. Although Notaries are authorized to take them, depositions are typically done by skilled court reporters. (See pages 29–30.)

- Verifications Upon Oath or Affirmation, as in depositions and affidavits, certifying that the signer personally appeared before the Notary, was positively identified, took an oath or affirmation, and signed a written statement in the Notary's presence. (See pages 30–31.)

- Witnessing Signatures, certifying that a signer personally appeared before the Notary, was positively identified and signed the document in the Notary's presence. (See pages 31–32.)

- **Oaths and Affirmations**, which are solemn promises to God (oaths) or solemn promises on one's own personal honor (affirmations). (See pages 32–34.)

- **Proofs of Acknowledgment by Subscribing Witness.** Although Washington Notary law does not address the use of proofs of execution, state officials say that Notaries may perform this type of act but should proceed with caution. (See pages 34–35.)

- **Certifying an Event or Act**, attesting that an event or act has occurred or has been performed. (See pages 35–36.)

- **Protests**, certifying that a negotiable instrument or other written promise to pay, such as a bill of exchange, was not honored. (See pages 36–38.)

Unauthorized Acts

Notary's Own Signature. Notaries are not permitted to notarize their own signatures. (RCW 42.44.080)

Marriages. Washington Notaries are not authorized to perform marriages unless the Notary is also a member of the clergy or an official authorized to solemnize marriages.

Testimonials or Endorsements. A Notary may not use the official Notary seal or the title "Notary Public" to endorse or promote any product or service. (WAC 308-30-160)

Telephone Notarizations. Notarizations over the telephone are forbidden. Washington law stipulates that a document signer *must* personally appear before the Notary at the time of notarization. Notarization based on a Notary's recognition of a signature without the signer's appearance is not permitted. (RCW 42.44.080)

Acknowledgments

A Common Notarial Act. Acknowledgments are one of the most common forms of notarization. Typically, they are executed on deeds and other documents affecting real property that will be publicly recorded by a county auditor.

Purpose. In executing an acknowledgment, the Notary

certifies three things: (RCW 42.44.080)

1) The signer *personally appeared* before the Notary on the date and in the county indicated on the notarial certificate (notarization cannot be based on a telephone call or on a Notary's familiarity with a signature); and

2) The signer was *positively identified* by the Notary through personal knowledge or other satisfactory evidence (see "Identifying Document Signers," pages 38–39); and

3) The signer *acknowledged* to the Notary that the signature was freely made for the purposes stated in the document. (If a document is willingly signed in the presence of the Notary, this tacit act can serve just as well as an oral statement of acknowledgment.)

Signing in Representative Capacity. A person may acknowledge the signature on a document as a representative of another person (e.g., as an attorney in fact) or of an impersonal legal entity (e.g., as a corporate officer).

The following representative capacities are recognized by Washington law: (RCW 42.44.010)

1) An authorized officer, agent, partner, trustee or other representative on behalf of a corporation, partnership, trust or other entity;

2) A public officer, personal representative, guardian or other representative in a capacity specified in the document;

3) An attorney in fact for a principal signer; and

4) An authorized representative of another person in any other capacity.

Proof of Representative Capacity. The Notary is encouraged to ask for proof of a person's authority to sign in a representative capacity. However, an acknowledgment certificate that indicates that the signer took an oath or affirmation declaring that he or she had authority to sign is generally recognized as significant proof of the person's authority to sign as a representative. (RCW

42.44.010, 42.44.100 and 64.08.070)

<u>Identifying the Representative Signer</u>. The Notary should identify the representative signer as any other signer: through personal knowledge, ID or the oath of a credible witness. Ideally, the person should also present some type documentary evidence granting that person authority to sign as a representative.

<u>Certificates for Acknowledgments</u>. Washington law provides wording for acknowledgment certificates that accommodate signers in individual and corporate capacities. (RCW 64.08.060 and 64.08.070)

- Certificate of acknowledgment for a person signing as an individual — wording must be substantially as follows:

State of Washington   )
County of _____)

On this day personally appeared before me _____ (name of person appearing), to me known to be the individual, or individuals, described in and who executed the within and foregoing instrument, and acknowledged that he/she/they signed the same as his/her/their free and voluntary act and deed, for the uses and purposes therein mentioned.
Given under my hand and official seal this _____ day of _____ (month), _____ (year).

_____ (Signature of Notary)   (Seal/Stamp of Notary)
Notary Public in and for the state of Washington, residing at _____ (Notary's residence).

- Certificate of acknowledgment for a person signing as a representative of a corporation — wording must be substantially as follows:

State of Washington   )
County of _____)

On this _____ day of _____ (month), _____ (year), before me personally appeared _____ (name of person appearing), to me known to be the _____ (title of corporate officer) of the corporation that executed the within and foregoing instrument, and acknowledged said instrument to be the free and voluntary act and deed of said corporation, for the uses and purposes therein mentioned, and on oath stated that he/she was authorized to execute said instrument and that the seal affixed is the corporate seal of said corporation.
In Witness Whereof I have hereunto set my hand and affixed my

official seal the day and year first above written.

_____ (Signature of Notary) (Seal/Stamp of Notary)
Notary Public in and for the state of Washington, residing at
_____ (Notary's residence).

<u>Short-Form Certificates</u>. The following short-form acknowledgment wording may be used in lieu of the lengthier versions set out on page 25. A Notary may use either the short- or long-form versions, depending on the circumstances. (RCW 42.44.100)

- Certificate of acknowledgment for a person signing as an individual — wording must be substantially as follows:

State of Washington)
County of _____)

I certify that I know or have satisfactory evidence that _____ (name of person) is the person who appeared before me, and said person acknowledged that he/she signed this instrument and acknowledged it to be his/her free and voluntary act for the uses and purposes mentioned in the instrument.
Dated: _____

_____ (Signature of Notary) (Seal/Stamp of Notary)
Notary Public — State of Washington
My Appointment Expires: _____

- Certificate of acknowledgment for a person signing as a representative (e.g. attorney in fact, corporate officer, etc.) — wording must be substantially as follows:

State of Washington)
County of _____)

I certify that I know or have satisfactory evidence that _____ (name of person) is the person who appeared before me, and said person acknowledged that he/she signed this instrument, on oath stated that he/she was authorized to execute the instrument and acknowledged it as the _____ (type of authority, e.g., attorney in fact, officer, etc.) of _____ (name of party or entity on behalf of whom the instrument was executed) to be the free and voluntary act of such party for the uses and purposes mentioned in the instrument.
Dated: _____

_____ (Signature of Notary) (Seal/Stamp of Notary)
Notary Public — State of Washington
My Appointment Expires: _____

Identification of Acknowledger. In executing an acknowledgment, the Notary must identify the signer through personal knowledge or another form of satisfactory evidence. (See "Identifying Document Signers," pages 38–41.) (RCW 42.44.080)

Witnessing Signature Not Required. For an acknowledgment, the document does *not* have to be signed in the Notary's presence. As long as the signer appears before the Notary at the time of notarization to *acknowledge having signed*, the Notary may execute the acknowledgment. The document could have been signed an hour before, a week before, a year before, etc. — as long as the signer appears before the Notary with the signed document at the time of notarization to admit that the signature is his or her own. (RCW 42.44.080)

Terminology. In discussing the notarial act of acknowledgment, it is important to use the proper terminology. A Notary *takes* or *executes* an acknowledgment, while a document signer *makes* or *gives* an acknowledgment.

Who May Take Acknowledgments. Besides Notaries, the following people may take acknowledgments in Washington: (RCW 64.08.010 and 64.08.090)

1) A justice, deputy or clerk of the supreme court;

2) A judge or clerk of a court of appeals;

3) A judge, court commissioner or clerk of a superior court;

4) A county auditor or deputy county auditor;

5) A qualified U.S. commissioner appointed by any district court of the United States for the state of Washington, or;

6) Certain officers of correctional institutions, provided that notarial acts are only performed for officers, employees and residents of the particular institution or facility.

Outside of Washington, but inside the United States and its jurisdictions, acknowledgments may be executed by: (RCW 42.44.130 and 64.08.020)

1) A Notary in other U.S. states and jurisdictions;

2) A judge, clerk or deputy clerk of a court; and

3) Any other person authorized in that jurisdiction.

Acknowledgments may be executed under federal authority by: (RCW 42.44.130)

1) A judge, clerk or deputy clerk of a court;

2) A commissioned officer on active duty with the U.S. Armed Forces;

3) An officer of the foreign service or a consular officer of the United States; and

4) Any other person authorized by U.S. federal or foreign law.

Outside of the United States and its jurisdictions, acknowledgments may be executed under foreign authority by: (RCW 42.44.130 and 64.08.040)

1) A Notary of that jurisdiction;

2) A judge, clerk or deputy clerk of a court; or

3) Any other person authorized in that jurisdiction.

Certified Copies

Purpose. Washington Notaries have authority to certify — or "attest" — that a copy of an original document is a complete and true reproduction of the document that was copied. The Notary should not certify copies of documents that are public records or recordable in the public records. (RCW 42.44.010)

Procedure. The custodian of the document must present it to the Notary and request a certified copy. A certified copy does not have to be made from an original document; a photocopy may serve as the original as long as it is so described (e.g., "a photocopy of a Univ. of Washington B.A. degree").

A common request is to certify a copy of a college diploma,

since only one such document exists and most people do not want to risk parting with the original when proof of their graduate status is requested by a prospective employer or school.

Precautions. Though a transcription or hand-rendered copy is permitted under Washington law, the NNA strongly recommends that Notaries only certify photocopies — rather than a transcribed copy in which the Notary hand-copies the text — to avert the high likelihood that something may be inadvertently omitted or mistranscribed in a handmade copy. And, to minimize the opportunity for fraud, the making of the photocopy should be done or supervised by the Notary. Otherwise, the Notary should carefully compare the copy to the original, word for word, to ensure that it is complete and identical. (RCW 42.44.080)

Copy Certification of Vital Records. Washington Notaries should not certify copies of birth, death or marriage certificates or divorce decrees, or of any other vital record. A Notary's "certification" of such a copy may lend credibility to what is actually a counterfeit or altered document. Only officials in a bureau of vital statistics or other public record office may certify originals or copies of such certificates and documents. (See "Bureaus of Vital Statistics," pages 106–110.)

Certificate for Certified Copy. Washington statute provides the following short-form certificate wording for certifying a copy of a document: (RCW 42.44.100)

    State of Washington   )
    County of _____)

    I certify that this is a true and correct copy of a document in the possession of _____ (name of person presenting document) as of this date.
    Dated: _____

    _____ (Signature of Notary)   (Seal/Stamp of Notary)
    Notary Public — State of Washington
    My Appointment Expires: _____

Depositions

Purpose. Although Washington law does permit any Notary to take depositions — meaning, to transcribe the words spoken aloud by a deponent — this duty is most often executed by

WASHINGTON NOTARY LAW PRIMER

Notaries who are trained and certified shorthand reporters, also known as court reporters. (RCW 5.28.010)

A deposition is a signed transcript of the signer's oral statements taken down for use in a judicial proceeding. The deposition signer is called the *deponent*.

With a deposition, both sides in a lawsuit or court case have the opportunity to question the deponent. The questions and answers are transcribed into a written statement, then signed and sworn to before an oath-administering official.

Wording for Deposition Oath (Affirmation). Washington statutes prescribe the following wording to administer to a deponent: (RCW 5.28.020 and 5.28.040)

> You do solemnly swear (affirm) that the evidence you shall give in the issue (or matter) now pending between _____ and _____ shall be the truth, the whole truth, and nothing but the truth, so help you God."

If the oath is to be administered to a person other than a witness giving testimony, the wording may be: (RCW 5.28.020)

> You do solemnly swear you will true answers make to such questions you may be asked.

Verification Upon Oath or Affirmation

Jurat Typically Part of Verification. In notarizing affidavits, depositions and other forms of written verification requiring an oath by the signer, the Notary typically executes a jurat. (RCW 42.44.010 and 42.44.080)

Purpose. While the purpose of an acknowledgment is to positively identify a document signer, the purpose of a verification with jurat is to compel truthfulness by appealing to the signer's conscience and fear of criminal penalties for perjury. In executing a jurat, a Notary certifies that: (42.44.080)

1) The signer *personally appeared* before the Notary at the time of notarization on the date and in the county indicated (notarization based on a telephone call or on familiarity with a signature is not acceptable); and

2) The person making the verification *affixed a signature* to

the document in the Notary's presence;

3) The Notary *administered an oath* or affirmation to the signer; and

4) The signer was *positively identified* by the Notary.

Certificate for a Verification. Certificate wording for a verification upon oath or affirmation is typically jurat wording. Washington law prescribes the following wording for a verification: (RCW 42.44.100)

> State of Washington   )
> County of _____)
>
> Signed and sworn to (or affirmed) before me on _____ (date) by _____ (name of person making statement).
>
> _____ (Signature of Notary)   (Seal/Stamp of Notary)
> Notary Public — State of Washington
> My Appointment Expires: _____

Identification. When executing a verification upon oath or affirmation, the Notary must positively identify each signer. (RCW 42.44.080)

Wording for Jurat Oath (Affirmation). If not otherwise prescribed by law, a Washington Notary may use the following or similar wording to administer an oath (or affirmation) in conjunction with a jurat:

> Do you solemnly swear that the statements in this document are true to the best of your knowledge and belief, so help you God?
>
> (Do you solemnly affirm that the statements in this document are true to the best of your knowledge and belief?)

Witnessing or Attesting a Signature

Purpose. The act of witnessing — or "attesting" — a signature is similar to a jurat, except that it does not require the signer to take an oath or affirmation.

In witnessing or attesting a signature, the Notary certifies that: (RCW 42.44.080)

1) The signer *personally appeared* before the Notary on the

date and in the county indicated on the notarial certificate;

2) The signer was *positively identified* by personal knowledge or satisfactory evidence; and

3) The signer *affixed the signature* in the presence of the Notary.

Certificate. A Notary may use the following short-form certificate for witnessing or attesting a signature: (RCW 42.44.100)

```
State of Washington    )
County of _____ )

Signed or attested before me on _____ (date) by _____ (name
of person appearing).

_____ (Signature of Notary)        (Seal/Stamp of Notary)
Notary Public — State of Washington
My Appointment Expires: _____
```

Oaths and Affirmations

Purpose. An oath is a solemn, spoken pledge to a Supreme Being. An affirmation is a solemn, spoken pledge on one's own personal honor, with no reference to a Supreme Being. Both are usually a promise or pledge of truthfulness or fidelity and have the same legal effect. In taking an oath or affirmation in an official proceeding, a person may be subject to criminal penalties for perjury should he or she fail to be truthful.

An oath or affirmation can be a full-fledged notarial act in its own right, as when giving an oath of office to a public official (when "swearing in" a public official), or it can be part of the process of notarizing a document (e.g., executing a jurat or swearing in a credible identifying witness).

A person who objects to taking an oath — pledging to a Supreme Being — may instead be given an affirmation, which does not refer to a Supreme Being.

Power to Administer. Washington Notaries and certain other officers are authorized to administer oaths and affirmations. (RCW 42.44.010)

Corporate Oaths Prohibited. A person may not take an oath or affirmation on behalf of a legal entity such as a corporation, partnership or other artificial signer. An oath or affirmation, as required by a verification or jurat, is a personal commitment of conscience that may only be taken by a human being.

However, notarial certificates may direct Notaries to administer an oath to a corporate signer to compel the person to be truthful about having the authority to sign. In such instances, it is the individual taking the oath, not the entity.

<u>Wording for Oath (Affirmation)</u>. If law does not dictate otherwise, a Washington Notary may use the following or similar words in administering an oath (or affirmation):

- Oath (affirmation) for an affiant signing an affidavit or a deponent signing a deposition:

   Do you solemnly swear that the statements in this document are true to the best of your knowledge and belief, so help you God?

   (Do you solemnly affirm that the statements in this document are true to the best of your knowledge and belief?)

- Oath (affirmation) for a credible identifying witness identifying a document signer who is in the Notary's presence:

   Do you solemnly swear that you personally know this signer truly holds the identity he (or she) claims, so help you God?

   (Do you solemnly affirm that you personally know this signer truly holds the identity he [or she] claims?)

<u>Response Required</u>. The oath or affirmation wording must be spoken aloud. The person taking the oath or affirmation must answer affirmatively with "I do," "Yes," or the like. A nod or grunt is not a sufficient response. If a person is mute and unable to speak, the Notary may rely on written notes to communicate.

<u>Ceremony and Gestures</u>. To impress upon the oath- or affirmation-taker the importance of truthfulness, the Notary is encouraged to lend a sense of ceremony and formality to the oath or affirmation. During administration of an oath or affirmation, the Notary and document signer traditionally raise their right hands, though this is not a legal requirement. Notaries generally have discretion to use words and gestures they feel

will most compellingly appeal to the conscience of the oath-taker or affirmant.

Proof of Acknowledgment by Subscribing Witness

Purpose. Typically, in executing a proof of acknowledgment by subscribing witness (also called a proof of execution by a subscribing witness), a Notary certifies that the signature of a person who does not appear before the Notary — the principal signer — is genuine and freely made based on the sworn testimony of another person who does appear — a subscribing (signing) witness.

There is no provision in Washington's Notary law that recognizes a proof of execution as an official notarial act, but state officials say that Notaries may indeed perform these proofs but should proceed with caution.

In Lieu of Acknowledgment. On recordable real estate documents, a proof of execution is typically regarded as an acceptable substitute for an acknowledgment. The signer should check with his or her real estate professional to see if this is appropriate in a specific instance.

Subscribing Witness. A subscribing witness is a person who watches a principal sign a document (or who personally takes the principal's acknowledgment) and then subscribes (signs) his or her own name on the document at the principal's request. This witness brings that document to a Notary on the principal's behalf and takes an oath or affirmation from the Notary to the effect that the principal did indeed willingly sign (or acknowledge signing) the document and request the witness to also sign the document.

The ideal subscribing witness personally knows both the Notary and the principal signer and has no personal beneficial or financial interest in the document or transaction. It would be foolish of the Notary, for example, to rely on the word of a subscribing witness presenting for notarization a power of attorney that names this very witness as attorney in fact.

Oath (Affirmation) for Subscribing Witness. An acceptable oath for the subscribing witness might be:

> Do you solemnly swear that you saw (name of the document signer) sign his/her name to this document and that he/she acknowledged to

you having executed it for the purposes therein stated, so help you God?

(Do you solemnly affirm that you saw [name of the document signer] sign his/her name to this document and that he/she acknowledged to you having executed it for the purposes therein stated?)

The subscribing witness then signs the Notary's journal, if one is kept, and the Notary completes a proof of execution by subscribing witness certificate, often called a "witness jurat."

Identifying Subscribing Witness. Because of the high potential for fraud with this type of notarization, it is recommended that the subscribing witness be personally known to the Notary. Less preferred is identification of the subscribing witness through satisfactory evidence — identification cards or credible witness.

Certificate for Proof of Execution. If no wording is provided, the National Notary Association recommends the following format for a proof of execution by a subscribing witness:

State of Washington
County of _____

On _____ (date), before me, the undersigned, a Notary Public for the state, personally appeared _____ (subscribing witness's name), personally known to me (or proved to me on the basis of _____ [identification method]), to be the person whose name is subscribed to the within instrument, as a witness thereto, who, being by me duly sworn, deposed and said that he/she was present and saw _____ (name of principal), the same person described in and whose name is subscribed to the within and annexed instrument in his/her authorized capacity(ies) as a party thereto, execute the same, and that said affiant subscribed his/her name to the within instrument as a witness at the request of _____ (name of principal).

_____ (Signature of Notary)   (Seal/Stamp of Notary)
Notary Public — State of Washington
My Appointment Expires: _____

Certification of an Event or Act

Purpose. Washington Notaries have the authority to certify that an event has occurred or an act has been performed. The Notary must determine the occurrence or performance, whether from personal knowledge or from satisfactory evidence based upon the oath or affirmation of a credible witness personally known to the Notary. (RCW 42.44.080)

Document Required. This type of certification should only be used in conjunction with an attached document. The Notary is verifying an event or act described in the document. Since Notaries should be impartial, it is recommended that they not certify events or acts involving themselves (e.g., the Notary mailing a check) — this would be similar to a Notary notarizing his or her own signature. (RCW 42.44.100)

Procedures. There are few official guidelines about how to perform this type of notarization, but the National Notary Association recommends the following:

1) Notaries should not use this type of notarization to endorse any commercial products, services or contests. Endorsements or testimonials by Notaries are strictly prohibited by Washington law. (WAC 308-30-160)

2) Notaries should only certify events or acts that do not require value judgments on the Notary's part. For example, this notarization might be used to certify that someone has mailed a package on a certain date. It should not be used to certify that someone is a person of "good character."

Certificate. Washington statutes prescribe the following short-form certificate: (RCW 42.44.100)

State of Washington   )
County of _____)

I certify that the event or act described in this document has occurred or been performed.

_____ (Signature of Notary)   (Seal/Stamp of Notary)
Notary Public — State of Washington
My Appointment Expires: _____

Protests

Purpose. In rare instances, Washington Notaries may be asked to protest a negotiable instrument for nonpayment. A protest is a written statement by a Notary or other authorized officer verifying that payment was not received on an instrument such as a bank draft. Failure to pay is called *dishonor.* Before issuing a certificate of protest, the Notary must present the bank draft or other instrument to the person, firm or institution obliged to pay, a procedure called *presentment*. (RCW 62A.3-501 to 62A.3-503 and 62A.3-505)

Antiquated Act. In the 19th century, protests were common notarial acts in the United States, but they rarely are performed today due to the advent of modern electronic communications and resulting changes in our banking and financial systems. Modern Notaries most often encounter protests in the context of international commerce.

Special Knowledge Required. Notarial acts of protest are complicated and varied, requiring a special knowledge of financial and legal terminology. Only Notaries who have the requisite special knowledge, or who are acting under the supervision of an experienced bank officer or an attorney familiar with the Uniform Commercial Code, should attempt a protest.

Certificate. Washington law prescribes the following wording for execution of a notice of dishonor. The notice of dishonor should be sent by mail to the drawer at the drawer's last known address, and the notice should be substantially in the following form: (RCW 62A.3-520 and 62A.3-522)

NOTICE OF DISHONOR OF CHECK

A check drawn by you and made payable by you to _____ in the amount of _____ has not been accepted for payment by _____, which is the drawee bank designated on your check. This check is dated _____, and it is numbered, No._____.

You are CAUTIONED that unless you pay the amount of this check within fifteen days after the date this letter is postmarked, you may very well have to pay the following additional amounts:
(1) Costs of collecting the amount of the check, including an attorney's fee which will be set by the court;
(2) Interest on the amount of the check which shall accrue at the rate of twelve percent per annum from the date of dishonor; and
(3) Three hundred dollars or three times the face amount of the check, whichever is less, by award of the court.
You are also CAUTIONED that law enforcement agencies may be provided with a copy of this notice of dishonor and the check drawn by you for the possibility of proceeding with criminal charges if you do not pay the amount of this check within fifteen days after the date this letter is postmarked.

You are advised to make your payment to _____ at the following address:_____

In addition to sending a notice of dishonor to the drawer of the check under RCW 62A.3-520, the holder of the check should execute an affidavit certifying service of the notice by mail. The affidavit of service by mail must be attached to a copy of the notice of dishonor and must be substantially in the following form:

AFFIDAVIT OF SERVICE BY MAIL
I, _____, hereby certify that on the _____ day of _____ (month), ____ (year), a copy of the foregoing Notice was served on _____ by mailing via the United States Postal Service, postage prepaid, at _____, Washington.
Dated: _____
_____ (Signature)

The holder must retain the affidavit with the check but must also file a copy of the affidavit with the clerk of the court in which an action on the check is commenced. (RCW 62A.3-522)

PRACTICES AND PROCEDURES

Identifying Document Signers

Acknowledgments and Jurats. Washington law requires the Notary to positively identify the signer for all notarial acts except for copy certifications and protests. The following three methods of identification are acceptable: (RCW 42.44.080 and WAC 308-30-155)

1) The Notary's *personal knowledge* of the signer's identity (see "Personal Knowledge of Identity," page 39);

2) The oath or affirmation of a personally known *credible identifying witness* (see "Credible Identifying Witnesses," pages 39–40); or

3) Reliable, current *identification documents* or ID cards (see "Identification Documents," pages 40–41).

Identification for Other Notarial Acts. While the law does not specify identification standards for copy certification and protests, the prudent and conscientious Notary will apply the above identification standards in identifying all persons requesting a notarial act.

Proof of Representative Capacity. The Notary is encouraged to ask for proof of a person's authority to sign in a representative capacity. However, an acknowledgment certificate indicating that the signer took an oath or affirmation declaring that he or she had authority to sign is generally regarded as sufficient proof of authority. (RCW 42.44.010)

Personal Knowledge of Identity

Definition. The safest and most reliable method of identifying a document signer is for the Notary to depend on his or her own personal knowledge of the signer's identity. Personal knowledge means familiarity with an individual resulting from interactions with that person over a period of time sufficient to eliminate every reasonable doubt that the person has the identity claimed. (RCW 42.44.080)

Washington law does not specify how long a Notary must be acquainted with an individual before personal knowledge of identity may be claimed. So, the Notary's common sense must prevail. In general, the longer the Notary is acquainted with a person, and the more random interactions the Notary has had with that person, the more likely the individual is indeed personally known.

For instance, the Notary might safely regard a friend since childhood as personally known, but would be foolish to consider a person met for the first time the previous day as such. Whenever the Notary has a reasonable doubt about a signer's identity, that individual should not be considered personally known, and the identification should be made through either a credible identifying witness or reliable identification documents.

Credible Identifying Witnesses

Purpose. When a document signer is not personally known to the Notary and is not able to present reliable ID cards, that signer may be identified on the oath (or affirmation) of a credible identifying witness ("credible witness"). (RCW 42.44.080 and WAC 308-30-155)

Qualifications. A credible identifying witness should be personally known to the Notary (though this is not stipulated in Washington law), and the document signer, as required by statute, must be personally known to the credible identifying witness. (See "Personal Knowledge of Identity," preceding.)

There should be a chain of personal knowledge linking the Notary to the credible identifying witness to the signer. In a sense, a credible identifying witness is a walking, talking ID card. (RCW 42.44.080 and WAC 308-30-155)

A reliable credible identifying witness should have a reputation for honesty. The witness should be a capable individual who would not be tricked, cajoled, bullied or otherwise influenced into identifying someone he or she does not really know. And the witness, ideally, should have no personal beneficial or financial interest in the transaction requiring a notarial act.

Oath (Affirmation) for Credible Identifying Witness. An oath or affirmation must be administered to the credible identifying witness by the Notary to compel truthfulness.

If not otherwise prescribed by law, a Washington Notary may use the following or similar wording to administer an oath (or affirmation) to credible identifying witnesses:

> Do you solemnly swear that you know the signer truly holds the identity he (or she) claims, so help you God?
>
> (Do you solemnly affirm that you know the signer truly holds the identity he [or she] claims?)

Journal Entry. If the Notary keeps a journal, each credible identifying witness's name and residence address should be recorded. Prudent Notaries will also ask witnesses to sign the journal.

Not a Subscribing Witness. Do not confuse a *credible identifying* witness with a *subscribing* witness. A credible identifying witness vouches for the identity of a signer who appears before the Notary. A subscribing witness vouches for the genuineness of the signature of a signer who does not appear before the Notary. (See "Proof of Acknowledgment by Subscribing Witness," pages 34–35.)

Identification Documents (ID Cards)

Acceptable Identification Documents. Washington requires that an identifying document or card relied on by a Notary to identify a stranger must be current and issued by a federal or a state governmental agency and must contain a photograph, physical description and signature of the bearer. (RCW 42.44.080 and WAC 308-30-155)

Multiple Identification. Identification documents that meet the criteria described above are sufficient to identify a signer. However, a Notary may ask for additional identification, especially if the Notary suspects fraud. (See "Fraudulent Identification," below)

Fraudulent Identification. Identification documents are the least secure of the three methods of identifying a document signer, because phony ID cards are common. The Notary should scrutinize each card for evidence of tampering or counterfeiting, or for evidence that it is a genuine card issued to an impostor.

Some clues that an ID card may have been fraudulently tampered with include: mismatched type styles, a photograph raised from the surface, a signature that does not match the signature on the document, unauthorized lamination of the card, and smudges, erasures, smears or discolorations.

Possible tip-offs to a counterfeit ID card include: misspelled words, a brand new-looking card with an old date of issuance, two cards with exactly the same photograph, and inappropriate patterns and textures.

Some possible indications that a card may have been issued to an impostor include: the card's birth date or address is unknown to the bearer, all the ID cards seem brand new, and the bearer is unwilling to leave a thumbprint in the journal. (Such a print is not a requirement of law but is requested by some Notaries as protection against forgers and lawsuits. Refusal to leave a thumbprint is not in itself grounds to deny a notarization.)

Journal of Notarial Acts and Notarial Records

Recommendation. The National Notary Association *strongly* recommends that every Notary keep a detailed, accurate and sequential journal of notarial acts even though it is not required by Washington law.

A journal record of a transaction demonstrates that the Notary used reasonable care in identifying a document signer. Failure to keep a journal, while not unlawful, can cause problems for a Notary if a transaction is challenged for any reason.

A permanently bound recordbook (not loose-leaf) with numbered pages and entry spaces is best for preserving the sequence of notarial acts and for protecting against unauthorized removal of pages or tampering.

Journal Entries. For each notarization, the following vital information should be recorded:

1) The date, time of day, and type of notarization (e.g., jurat, acknowledgment, etc.);

2) The date and type of document notarized (e.g., deed of trust, affidavit of support, etc.);

3) The printed name, address, and the signature of each person whose signature is notarized; the signature of any credible or subscribing witness; and the signature of any witnesses to a signature by mark.

4) A statement as to how the signer's identity was confirmed (If by personal knowledge, the journal entry should read "Personal Knowledge." If by satisfactory evidence, the journal entry should contain either: a description of the ID card accepted, including the type of ID, the government agency issuing the ID, the serial or identifying number, and the date of issuance or expiration; or the signature of each credible identifying witness and how the credible identifying witness was identified — see "Credible Identifying Witness(es)," pages 39–40); and

5) The fee charged for the notarial service.

Additional Entries. Notaries may include additional information in their journals that is pertinent to a given notarization. Many Notaries, for example, enter the telephone number of all other signers and witnesses, as well as the address where the notarization was performed, if not at the Notary's office. A description of the document signer's demeanor (e.g., "The signer appeared very nervous") or notations about the identity of other persons who were present for the notarization may also be pertinent.

One important entry to include is the signer's representative capacity — whether the signer is acting as attorney in fact, trustee, guardian, corporate officer or in another capacity — if not signing on his or her own behalf.

Increasingly, Notaries are asking document signers to leave a thumbprint in the journal as a deterrent to fraud, since no forger wants to leave a print behind as evidence of an attempted crime.

Since a journal record of a notarial act is not required by law, refusal to leave a signature or fingerprint in the journal is not in itself sufficient grounds for the Notary to refuse to honor an otherwise lawful and reasonable request for a notarization.

Journal-Entry Copies. A Notary's official journal is a public record. Accordingly, if any person submits a written request specifying the month and year of a particular notarization, as well as the type of document and the names of the signers, the Notary may provide that person with a photocopy of the particular entry in the journal — but of no other entries! Adjacent entries should be covered by a sheet of blank paper before the photocopy is made.

The National Notary Association discourages "fishing expeditions" through the Notary journal by persons who are not able to be specific about the entry sought.

Never Surrender Journal. Notaries should never surrender control of their journals to anyone, unless expressly subpoenaed by a court order. Even when an employer has paid for the Notary's journal and seal, they go with the Notary upon termination of employment; no person but the Notary can lawfully possess and use these official tools of office.

Notarial Certificate

Requirement. In notarizing any document, a Notary must complete a notarial certificate. The certificate is wording that indicates exactly what the Notary has certified. The notarial certificate may be typed or printed on the document itself or on an attachment to it. (RCW 42.44.090)

The certificate should contain: (RCW 42.44.090 and WAC 308-30-120)

> 1) A *venue* indicating where the notarization is being performed. "State of Washington, County of _____," is the typical venue wording, with the appropriate county inserted in the blank. The letters "SS." or "SCT." sometimes appear after the venue; they abbreviate the Latin word *scilicet*, meaning "in particular" or "namely."

2) A *statement of particulars* which indicates what the notarization has certified. An acknowledgment certificate would include such wording as: "This instrument was acknowledged before me on _____ (date) by _____ (name of signer)." A jurat certificate would include such wording as: "Signed and sworn to (or affirmed) before me on _____ (date) by _____ (name of signer)."

3) A *testimonium clause*, which may be optional if the date is included in the statement of particulars: "Witness my hand and official seal, this _____ day of _____ (month), _____ (year)." In this phrase, the Notary formally attests to the truthfulness of the preceding facts in the certificate. "Hand" means signature.

4) The *official signature of the Notary*, exactly as the name appears on the appointment certificate and on the Notary's official seal/stamp.

5) The *official seal of the Notary*. On many certificates, the letters "L.S." appear, indicating where the Notary's seal is to be placed. These letters abbreviate the Latin term *locus sigilli*, meaning "place of the seal." An inking stamp should be placed near but not over the letters, so that wording imprinted by the stamp will not be obscured. An embossing seal may be affixed over the letters.

<u>Loose Certificates</u>. When appropriate certificate wording is not preprinted on the document for the Notary to fill out, a "loose" certificate may be attached. Normally, this form is stapled to the document's left margin on the signature page. Only one side of the certificate should be stapled, so it can be lifted to view the document beneath it.

To prevent a loose certificate from being removed and fraudulently placed on another document, there are precautions a Notary can take. For instance, the Notary can write a brief description of the document on the certificate: e.g., "This certificate is attached to a _____ (title or type of document), dated _____, of _____ (number) pages, also signed by _____ (name[s] of other signer[s])."

While fraud-deterrent steps such as this one can make it

much more difficult for a loose certificate to be removed and misused, there is no absolute protection against removal and misuse. Notaries, however, must absolutely ensure that while a certificate remains in their control, it is attached only to its intended document. A Notary must never give or mail a signed and stamped notarial certificate to another person and trust that person to attach it to a particular document; this would be an indefensible action in a civil court of law.

Must Be Page-Size. Effective January 1, 1997, no paper attachments bearing Notary certificate wording may be stapled, taped or glued to pages of a document that will be recorded by county auditors in Washington.

If appropriate notarial certificate wording (e.g., acknowledgment or jurat) is not printed or typed on the document itself, the certificate may only be attached if it is on a sheet exactly the same size as the document's other pages and fastened in the same way as are the other pages. The only exception to this rule applies to surveyed maps.

Documents with notarial forms that are less than a full page in size will be rejected by the county auditor. In addition, no document page or notarial certificate may be larger than 8½ by 14 inches. (RCW 65.04.045)

Must Have One-Inch Margin. Effective January 1, 1997, any document presented for recording in Washington state must have a one-inch margin on the top, bottom and sides of all pages, except the first page. The first page must have a top margin of at least three inches. Thus, any Notary certificate attached to a recordable document must not only be page-sized, but must also have a top, bottom and side margin of at least one inch. (RCW 65.04.045)

Effective June 11, 1998, county auditors will permit a Notary's seal, incidental writing or a minor portion of a signature to protrude into the margin. Such instances will not affect a document's recording. (RCW 65.04.045)

Type Not Less Than Eight Points. Effective January 1, 1997, no page or Notary certificate may contain printing in a typesize smaller than 8 points in size. (RCW 65.04.045)

Documents Not Recorded in Washington. Pages and Notary

certificates on documents that will not be recorded in Washington by a county auditor may not need to adhere to specified format requirements. However, to avoid an unintentional mistake, the National Notary Association encourages Washington Notaries to consistently use certificates that adhere to the new format, regardless of where the signer intends to record the document.

Selecting Certificates. Washington law specifically prohibits Notaries from selecting notarial certificates for any transaction. However, this does not prevent a Notary who is duly licensed and qualified in a particular field from giving advice relating to matters in that specific field. (WAC 308-30-090)

To be safe, if a document is presented to a Notary without certificate wording, and the signer cannot indicate what type of notarization (e.g., acknowledgment, verification, etc.) is appropriate, the NNA recommends that the signer be asked to find out what type of notarization and certificate are needed. Usually the agency that issued or will be accepting the document can provide this information.

Do Not Pre-Sign/Seal Certificates. A Notary should *never* sign or seal certificates ahead of time or permit other persons to attach loose notarial certificates to documents. Nor should the Notary send an unattached, signed and sealed, loose certificate through the mail, even if requested to do so by a signer who previously appeared before the Notary. These actions may facilitate fraud or forgery, and they could subject the Notary to lawsuits to recover damages resulting from the Notary's neglect or misconduct.

Short Form Certificates. Washington Notaries may use the following short-form certificates for the purposes indicated: (RCW 42.44.100)

• Acknowledgment by person signing in an individual capacity:

> State of Washington
> County of _____
>
> I certify that I know or have satisfactory evidence that (name of person) is the person who appeared before me, and said person acknowledged that he/she signed this instrument and acknowledged it

to be his/her free and voluntary act for the uses and purposes mentioned in the instrument.
Dated: _____

_____ (Signature of Notary)   (Seal/Stamp of Notary)
Notary Public — State of Washington
My Appointment Expires: _____

- **For an acknowledgment in a representative capacity:**

State of Washington   )
County of _____)

I certify that I know or have satisfactory evidence that (name of person) is the person who appeared before me, and said person acknowledged that he/she signed this instrument, on oath stated that he/she was authorized to execute the instrument and acknowledged it as the (type of authority, e.g., officer, trustee, etc.) of (name of party on behalf of whom instrument was executed) to be the free and voluntary act of such party for the uses and purposes mentioned in the instrument.
Dated: _____

_____ (Signature of Notary)   (Seal/Stamp of Notary)
Notary Public — State of Washington
My Appointment Expires: _____

- **For a verification upon oath or affirmation:**

State of Washington   )
County of _____)

Signed and sworn to (or affirmed) before me on _____ (date) by _____ (name[s] of person[s] making statement).

_____ (Signature of Notary)   (Seal/Stamp of Notary)
Notary Public — State of Washington
My Appointment Expires: _____

- **For witnessing or attesting a signature:**

State of Washington   )
County of _____)

Signed or attested before me on _____ (date) by _____ (name[s] of person[s]).

_____ (Signature of Notary)   (Seal/Stamp of Notary)
Notary Public — State of Washington
My Appointment Expires: _____

- For certifying or attesting a copy of a document:

    State of Washington   )
    County of _____)

    I certify that this is a true and correct copy of a document in the possession of _____ as of this date.
    Dated: _____

    _____ (Signature of Notary)   (Seal/Stamp of Notary)
    Notary Public — State of Washington
    My Appointment Expires: _____

- For certifying the occurrence of an event or the performance of an act:

    State of Washington   )
    County of _____)

    I certify that the event or act described in this document has occurred or been performed.
    Dated: _____

    _____ (Signature of Notary)   (Seal/Stamp of Notary)
    Notary Public — State of Washington
    My Appointment Expires: _____

False Certificate. A Notary Public who knowingly creates or completes a false notarial certificate may be guilty of a gross misdemeanor. (RCW 42.20.050 and 42.44.160)

In addition, a Notary who falsely completes a written instrument — for example, filling in a document's blank spaces — may be guilty of a Class C felony alleging forgery with intent to deceive or defraud. (RCW 9A.60.020)

Illegible Imprint or Writing. The illegibility of any wording, writing, marking, or seal or stamp impression on the document or certificate does not necessarily invalidate the notarization. (RCW 42.44.110)

Validity of Telegraphic Copies. Any instrument in writing that has been notarized may be transmitted by telegraph. The telegraphic copy shall be considered prima facie evidence to have the same validity and effect as if it were an original. The burden of proof shall rest on the party denying the genuineness of the document. (RCW 5.52.050)

Notary Seal or Stamp

<u>Authorization to Purchase Seal or Stamp</u>. When a Notary application has been approved, the Secretary of State sends the new Notary a Certificate of Appointment, a photocopy of which authorizes purchase of the required Notary seal or stamp. (RCW 42.44.050)

<u>Requirement</u>. A Washington Notary must affix an impression of an official seal or stamp on the certificate portion of every document notarized. However, a seal or stamp is not required in certifying an oath for use in any court in the state of Washington. The impression may not be placed over any signature or wording on a notarial certificate. The inking stamp must print in indelible black ink a photographically reproducible impression. A hand-drawn seal is not acceptable. (RCW 42.44.050, 42.44.090 and WAC 308-30-010)

<u>Format</u>. The inking stamp must be rectangular or circular. If it is rectangular, it must measure, at a minimum, 1 inch high and 1⅝ inches long. If it is circular, it must measure, at a minimum, 1⅝ inches in diameter.

The embossing seal must be circular, a minimum of 1⅝ inches in diameter. (WAC 308-30-010)

<u>Required Information</u>. The Notary seal or stamp must contain the following elements: (RCW 42.44.050 and WAC 308-30-010)

- The surname and at least the initials of the first and middle names of the Notary Public in not less than 8-point type;

- The words "Notary Public" and "State of Washington", printed in not less than 8-point type;

- The Notary's commission expiration date, printed in not less than 8-point type.

<u>Use of Expired Seal Prohibited</u>. Use of a Notary's seal or stamp with an expired date is expressly prohibited by law. (WAC 308-30-130)

<u>Use of State Seal Prohibited</u>. Use of the Washington State Seal on the Notary seal or stamp is forbidden. (WAC 308-30-010)

Embosser. Many Notaries use an embosser — called a "seal" in Washington statutes — *in addition* to the required photographically reproducible stamp, but it must not be used over this stamp nor over the Notary's signature.

The embosser may be affixed over the letters "L.S." — abbreviating the Latin term *locus sigilli*, meaning "location of the seal" — appear on many notarial certificates to indicate where the Notary seal should be placed.

Placement of the Seal/Stamp Impression. The Notary's official seal or stamp impression should be placed near, but not over, the Notary's signature on the notarial certificate. Should there be no room for a seal or stamp, the Notary may have no choice but to complete and attach a loose certificate that duplicates the notarial wording on the document.

Seal/Embosser Manufacturer. A seal or embosser vendor may not provide a person with a Notary seal or embosser without a photocopy of the person's Notary Certificate of Appointment. If a new seal or embosser is required due to a Notary's name change, the vendor must receive a copy of the new Certificate showing the change. (WAC 308-30-100)

Preprinted Seal Prohibited. The Notary's inking seal or embosser must contain permanently affixed letters and numbers, and may not be preprinted — for example, by computer or digital imaging. (WAC 308-30-010)

Lost or Stolen Seal or Stamp. If a Notary's seal or stamp is lost or stolen, the Notary must mail or deliver a written notice to the Department of Licensing by certified mail.

The notice must state that the seal or stamp has been lost or stolen, and it must be signed by the Notary. The Notary may then obtain a replacement seal or stamp which must contain some variance from the original seal or stamp (e.g., if only initials were used on the original, include full name on the replacement seal or stamp).

If the original seal or stamp is subsequently recovered after a replacement has been obtained, the original must be surrendered to the Department of Licensing. (WAC 308-30-050)

Disposition of the Notary's Seal or Stamp. Upon revocation

or resignation of the Notary's appointment, the Notary seal or stamp must be delivered to the Department of Licensing. (WAC 308-30-040)

When a Notary resigns the appointment, the Notary seal or stamp must be filed with the Secretary of State at the same time the Notary files the letter of resignation. (WAC 308-30-040)

When an appointment expires naturally after the four-year term, the Notary is not required to submit the seal or stamp to the Department of Licensing, but should destroy the seal or stamp as soon as possible to eliminate the chance of fraudulent misuse.

Should the Notary die during the commission term, the Notary's personal representative should destroy the seal or stamp. Any notarial records (e.g., the journal) should be retained for a reasonable amount of time, typically for the amount of time prescribed by the statute of limitations.

Seal/Embosser Sole Property of Notary. The Notary seal and embosser are the exclusive property of the Notary named on them and must not be used by any other person or surrendered to an employer upon termination of the Notary's employment, regardless of whether the employer paid for them. (RCW 42.44.090)

Fees for Notarial Services

Maximum Fees. The following maximum fees for performing notarial acts are allowed by Washington law: (WAC 308-30-020)

- Acknowledgments — $5. For taking an acknowledgment, the Notary may charge $5 for the first two people, and $5 for each additional person.

- Certified Copies — $5. For certifying a copy, the Notary may charge $5 for each certified copy certificate. However, for copying any instrument, a Notary may charge $1 for the first page and 25¢ for each additional page.

- Certifying an Event or Act — $5. For certifying that an event has occurred or an act has been preformed, the Notary may charge $5.

- Verification Upon Oath or Affirmation — $5. For executing a jurat on an affidavit or other form of verification upon oath or affirmation, the Notary may charge $5 for the first two people, and $5 for each additional person.

- Oaths and Affirmations — $5. For administering an oath or affirmation, the Notary may charge $5 per person.

- Witnessing or Attesting a Signature — $5. For witnessing or attesting a signature, the Notary may charge $5 per signature.

- Proof of Execution by Subscribing Witness — $5. Although not prescribed by law, state officials suggest that a Notary charge the same as for the performance of an acknowledgment: $5 for the first two people, and $5 for each additional person.

- Protests — $5. For protesting a bill or note, the fee is $5. However, if the Notary is required to be present at demand, tender, protest or deposit or noting the protest, an additional fee of $5, plus a mileage rate of $1 per mile may be charged.

Travel Fees. Charges for travel by a Notary are specified by law only for protests. For all other notarial acts, such fees are proper only if Notary and signer agree beforehand on the amount to be charged. The signer must understand that a travel fee is not stipulated in law and is separate from the notarial fees described above. (WAC 308-30-020)

Option Not to Charge. Notaries are not required to charge for their notarial services. And they may charge any fee less than the statutory maximum. (RCW 42.44.120 and WAC 308-30-020)

Overcharging. Charging more than the prescribed maximum fees is considered "requesting unlawful compensation," which is a Class C felony. (RCW 9A.68.020)

Posting of Fees. A Washington Notary who charges fees for notarial services is required to post in a conspicuous area at his or her place of business a notice of the fees allowed by law to be charged. The notice must be in English and be in at least 10-point type. (WAC 308-30-020)

Disqualifying Interest

Impartiality. Notaries are appointed by the state to be impartial, disinterested witnesses whose screening duties help ensure the integrity of important legal and commercial transactions. Lack of impartiality by a Notary throws doubt on the integrity and lawfulness of any transaction. A Notary must never notarize his or her own signature, or notarize in a transaction in which the Notary is named. (RCW 42.44.080)

Financial or Beneficial Interest. A Notary should not perform any notarization related to a transaction in which that Notary or the Notary's spouse has a direct financial or beneficial interest. A financial or beneficial interest exists when the Notary or the Notary's spouse is individually named as a principal in a financial transaction or when the Notary receives an advantage, right, privilege, property, or fee valued in excess of the lawfully prescribed notarial fee.

In regard to real estate transactions, a Notary is generally considered to have a disqualifying financial or beneficial interest when that Notary or the Notary's spouse is a grantor or grantee, a mortgagor or mortgagee, a trustor or trustee, a lessor or lessee, or a beneficiary in any way of the transaction.

Relatives. The National Notary Association strongly discourages Notaries from notarizing for persons related by blood or marriage, because of the likelihood of a financial or beneficial interest, whether large or small. And, of course, the Notary may not notarize if he or she is a party to or has signed the document. (RCW 42.44.080)

Refusal of Services

Legal Request for Services. Notaries must honor all lawful and reasonable requests to notarize. (RCW 42.20.100)

A person's race, gender, religion, nationality, ethnicity, lifestyle or politics is never legitimate cause for refusing to perform a notarial act. As a public servant, a Notary should treat all people fairly and equally.

Reasonable Care

Responsibility. As public servants, Notaries must act responsibly and exercise reasonable care in the performance of their official duties. If a Notary fails to do so, he or she may be subject to a civil suit to recover financial damages caused by the Notary's error or omission.

In general, reasonable care is that degree of concern and

attentiveness that a person of normal intelligence and responsibility would exhibit. If a Notary can show to a judge or jury that he or she did everything expected of a reasonable person, the judge or jury is obligated by law to find the Notary blameless and not liable for damages.

Complying with all pertinent laws is the first rule of reasonable care for a Notary. If there are no statutory guidelines in a given instance, the Notary should take all reasonable steps to use common sense and prudence. (See "Steps to Proper Notarization," pages 13–17.)

Blank or Incomplete Documents

<u>Against Common Sense</u>. While Washington law does not specifically address notarizing blank or incomplete documents, this dangerous, unbusinesslike practice is widely discouraged as a breach of common sense, similar to signing a blank check.

A fraudulent document could readily be created above a Notary's certificate on a blank paper. And, with documents containing blanks to be filled in after notarization, there is a danger that the information inserted later may be contrary to the wishes of the signer.

Employer/Notary Relationship

<u>Employer Does Not Own Commission</u>. Even when an employer has paid for a Notary's commissioning fees, seal, journal and supplies, the Notary's primary allegiance is to the laws of the State of Washington, not to the employer. (RCW 42.44.090)

Many employers and supervisors may ask a Notary to notarize the signature of a person who is not present, although this is a violation of law for which the Notary may be held civilly and criminally liable. Notaries must always remember that the primary responsibility and financial liability for performing an illegal or improper notarial act belongs exclusively to the Notary, although an employer may be penalized for coercing or threatening the Notary.

Unauthorized Practice of Law

<u>Do Not Assist with Legal Matters</u>. A Notary may not give legal advice or accept fees for legal advice. As a ministerial officer, a nonattorney Notary is generally not permitted to assist in drafting, preparing, completing or explaining a document or transaction.

The Notary should not fill in blank spaces in the text of a

document for other persons, tell others what documents they need nor how to draft them, nor advise others about the legal sufficiency of a document — and especially not for a fee.

A Notary, of course, may fill in the blanks on the portion of a document containing the notarial wording. And a Notary, as a private individual, may prepare legal documents to which he or she is personally a party; but the Notary may not then notarize his or her signature on those same documents.

Notaries who overstep their authority by advising others on legal matters may be guilty of a gross misdemeanor. Subsequent offenses may comprise a Class C felony. (RCW 2.48.170, 2.48.180 and WAC 308-30-090)

Exceptions. Nonattorney Notaries who are specially trained, certified or licensed in a particular field (e.g., real estate, insurance, escrow) may advise others about documents in that field, but in no other. In addition, trained paralegals under the supervision of an attorney may advise others about documents in routine legal matters. (WAC 308-30-090)

Signature by Mark

Mark Serves as Signature. A person who cannot sign his or her name because of illiteracy or a physical disability may instead use a mark — an "X" for example — as a signature, as long as there are witnesses to the making of the mark.

Witnesses for Notarization. For a signature by mark to be notarized, there should be two impartial witnesses, in addition to the Notary, to the making of the mark. Both witnesses should also sign the document, and one witness should write out the marker's name beside the mark. It is recommended that a mark also be affixed in the Notary's journal, if kept, and that the witnesses also sign the journal.

Notarization Procedures. Because a properly witnessed mark is regarded as a legal signature, no special procedures or certificates are required. The marker must be positively identified, as must any other signer, and regular notarial certificates may be used.

Notarizing for a Person Who Directs Another to Sign

Persons with a Disability. If a person cannot sign a document due to a physical disability, he or she may direct the Notary to sign on his or her behalf. (RCW 42.44.080 and 64.08.100)

Notarization. A Notary may notarize this signature but should take extra care to avoid any problems. As with any notarization, the Notary must determine the person's willingness and understanding of the nature and consequences of the transaction.

In addition, the Notary should positively identify the person through personal knowledge, a credible identifying witness or ID cards.

Certificate. The Notary's acknowledgment certificate must state the Notary's name and place of residence, and that the principal's signature was affixed under the authority of RCW 64.08.100. (RCW 42.44.080 and 64.08.100)

When no notarial wording is provided, the National Notary Association suggests the following wording:

> State of Washington   )
> County of _____)
>
> I certify that I know or have satisfactory evidence that _____ (name of person unable to sign) is the person who appeared before me and that said person was unable to write his/her name or to make a mark and appears otherwise capable, and that said person orally directed me to write his/her signature on this instrument on his/her behalf under authority of RCW 64.08.100, and acknowledged it to be his/her free and voluntary act for the uses and purposes mentioned in the attached instrument.
> Dated: _____
>
> _____ (Signature of Notary)   (Seal/Stamp of Notary)
> Notary Public — State of Washington
> My Appointment Expires: _____

Journal Entry. The prudent Notary will record the specific circumstances of the notarization in a journal. In addition, the Notary should note that he or she affixed the principal's signature under authority of RCW 64.08.100.

Marriages

No Authority to Perform. A Washington Notary does not have the authority to perform a marriage ceremony unless the person is also a member of the clergy or an official authorized to solemnize marriages. However, any person may obtain a marriage license by mail, execute it and acknowledge it before a

Notary. (RCW 26.04.150)

Notarizing for Minors

Under Age 18. Generally, persons must reach the age of majority before they can handle their own legal affairs and sign documents for themselves. In Washington, the age of majority is 18. Normally, natural guardians (parents) or court-appointed guardians will sign on a minor's behalf. In certain cases, minors may lawfully sign documents and have their signatures notarized — minors engaged in business transactions or children serving as court witnesses, for example.

Include Age Next to Signature. When notarizing for a minor, the Notary should ask the young signer to write his or her age next to the signature on the document and in the journal. This will alert any interested party that the signer is a minor. The Notary is not required to verify the minor signer's age.

Identification. The method for identifying a minor is the same as that for an adult. However, determining the identity of a minor can be a problem, because minors often do not possess acceptable identification documents, such as driver's licenses or passports. If the minor does not have an acceptable ID, then the other methods of identifying signers must be used, either the Notary's personal knowledge of the minor or the oath of a credible identifying witness who can identify the minor. (See "Identifying Document Signers," pages 38–41.)

Authentication

Documents Sent Out of State. Documents notarized in Washington and sent out of state may be required to bear proof that the Notary's signature and stamp are genuine and that the Notary had authority to act at the time of notarization. This process of proving the genuineness of an official signature and stamp is called *authentication* or *legalization*.

In Washington, the proof is in the form of an authenticating certificate attached to the notarized document by the Department of Licensing. Washington regulations prescribe that a person needing an authentication certificate contact the Department of Licensing directly. (RCW 42.44.180 and WAC 308-30-070)

Authenticating certificates are known by many different names: certificates of official character, certificates of authority, certificates of capacity, certificates of prothonotary and "flags."

The fee for an authenticating certificate is $15 per document (by check, payable to "Washington State Treasurer"). The certificate may be obtained by mail by writing to: Department of Licensing, Business & Occupations Unit, Notary Public Licensing Program, P.O. Box 9027, Olympia, WA 98507-9027. Additional information is available by calling 1-360-753-3836.

The original notarized document *must* be forwarded with the written request, the Notary's name and commission expiration date, and the fee. It is not the Notary's responsibility to pick up or pay for the certificate of authority.

Documents Sent Out of Country. If a notarized document will be sent out of the United States, a chain-authentication process may be necessary, and additional certificates of authority may have to be obtained from the U.S. Department of State and different ministries of a given foreign nation, here and abroad. This chain-certification process can be time-consuming and expensive. Contact the Department of Licensing at 1-360-753-3836 for more information.

Apostilles and the Hague Convention. Fortunately, over 50 nations, including the United States, subscribe to a treaty under auspices of the Hague Conference that simplifies authentication of notarized documents exchanged between any of these nations. The official name of this treaty, adopted by the Conference on October 5, 1961, is the Hague Convention Abolishing the Requirement of Legalization for Foreign Public Documents. For a list of the subscribing countries, see "Hague Convention Nations," pages 111–113.

Under the Hague Convention, only one authenticating certificate called an *apostille* is necessary to ensure acceptance of a Notary's signature and seal or stamp in these subscribing countries. (*Apostille* means "notation" in French.)

In Washington, *apostilles* are issued by the Department of Licensing. The fees and procedures are the same as for obtaining an ordinary authenticating certificate, except that the country for which the document is destined should also be specified in the written request. (RCW 42.44.180 and WAC 308-30-070)

Foreign Languages

Non-English Advertising. A nonattorney Notary advertising

notarial services in a foreign language must take steps to guard against misinterpretation of his or her function as a Notary. Notaries are encouraged to include in any such foreign language advertisement the following statement in English and the foreign language:

> 1) The statement: "I am not licensed to practice law in the State of Washington, and I am not permitted to give legal advice on immigration or other legal matters or accept fees for legal advice"; and
>
> 2) The statutory fees a Notary is allowed to charge.

Notaries are encouraged to include the above information when advertising with signs and all other forms of written communication (e.g., business cards, yellow page ads, Internet communication).

Furthermore, literal translation of "Notary Public" into Spanish (*Notario Publico* or *Notaria Publica*) or into any equivalent non-English term should be avoided to avert any misunderstanding by non-English speakers..

Foreign-Language Documents. Ideally, documents in foreign languages should be referred to Washington Notaries who read and write those languages. If not available in the general public, bilingual Notaries may be often found in foreign consulates.

Washington law does not directly address notarizing documents written in a language the Notary cannot read. Although notarizing such documents is not expressly prohibited, there are difficulties and dangers in notarizing any document the Notary cannot understand. The foremost danger is that the document may have been misrepresented to the Notary. The Notary cannot know if the document is false or endorses or promotes a product using the Notary seal and may unknowingly perform an illegal act or facilitate fraud by notarizing it.

If a Notary chooses to notarize a document that he or she cannot read, at the very least the notarial certificate should be in English, or in a language the Notary can read.

Foreign-Language Signers. There should always be direct communication between the Notary and document signer — whether in English or any other language. The Notary should never rely on an intermediary or interpreter to be assured that a signer is willing to execute a document and understands the significance of the transaction, since this third party may have a motive for misrepresenting the circumstances to the Notary and/or the signer.

Immigration

Do Not Give Advice. Nonattorney Notaries may never advise others on the subject of immigration, nor help others prepare immigration documents — and especially not for a fee. Notaries who offer immigration advice to others may be prosecuted for the unauthorized practice of law. (WAC 308-30-090)

Documents. Affidavits are the forms issued or accepted by the U.S. Immigration and Naturalization Service (INS) that most often require notarization, with the Affidavit of Support (I-134/I-864) being perhaps the most common. Non-INS-issued documents are often notarized and submitted in support of an immigration or naturalization petition. These might include translator's declarations, statements from employers and banks, and affidavits of relationship.

If there appears to be no room for the Washington Notary seal or stamp on an INS-issued document, federal officials advise that it may be affixed over boilerplate text (standard preprinted clauses or sections).

Naturalization Certificates. A Notary may be in violation of federal law if he or she makes a typewritten, photostatic, or any other type of copy of a certificate of naturalization or notarizes it. (U.S. Penal Code, Sec. 75 and U.S. Code, Title 18, Sec. 137)

Military-Personnel Notarizations

May Notarize Worldwide. Certain U.S. military personnel may notarize for military personnel and their dependents anywhere in the world. Under federal statutory authority, the following persons are authorized to act as Notaries:

- Civilian attorneys employed as legal assistance attorneys and licensed to practice law in the United States.

- Judge advocates on active duty or training as reservists on inactive duty.

- All adjutants, assistant adjutants, acting adjutants and personnel adjutants.

- Enlisted paralegals, personnel rank of E-4 or higher, on active duty or training on inactive duty.

- Active duty personnel who are commissioned officers or senior noncommissioned officers (rank E-7 or higher) who are stationed at a Geographically Separated Unit (GSU) or location where no authorized Notary official is available, and who are appointed in writing by the unit's servicing general courtmartial convening authority.

Certificate. When signing documents in their official capacity, military-officer Notaries must specify the date and location of the notarization, list their title and office, and use a raised seal or inked stamp citing Title 10 U.S.C. 1044a. (U.S. Code, Title 10, Sections 936, 1044a)

Authentication. Authentication of a military-officer notarization certificate is not required.

Wills

Do Not Offer Advice. Often, people attempt to draw up wills on their own without benefit of legal counsel and then bring these homemade testaments to a Notary to have them "legalized," expecting the Notary to know how to proceed. In advising or assisting such persons, the Notary risks prosecution for the unauthorized practice of law. The Notary's ill-informed advice may do considerable damage to the affairs of the signer and subject the Notary to a civil lawsuit to recover losses.

Wills are highly sensitive documents, the format of which is dictated by strict laws. The slightest deviation from these laws can nullify a will. In some cases, holographic (handwritten) wills have actually been voided by notarization because the document was not entirely in the handwriting of the testator.

Avoid the Unauthorized Practice of Law. In a memorandum to Washington Notaries, dated September 19, 1985, Attorney General Kenneth Eikenberry advised "that a Notary may notarize the signatures upon, and statements of witnesses to, wills in which the Notary has no beneficial interest and when the

Notary is not one of the persons whose signature or statement is being notarized.

"However, a Notary should not render advice upon legal questions, such as the validity of a will, the required form for a witness's statement, the number of witnesses required to make a will valid in this state, or the effectiveness of any of the provisions of the will. These types of questions should be referred to an attorney. If a Notary attempts to answer them, and the Notary is wrong resulting in loss or damage to any person, the Notary may be held to the standard of an attorney in any subsequent legal action. Further, depending upon the circumstances, the Notary may be found to have engaged in the unauthorized practice of law."

Do Not Proceed Without Certificate Wording. A Notary should notarize a document described as a will only if a notarial certificate is provided or stipulated for each signer, and the signers are not asking questions about how to proceed. Any such questions should properly be answered by an attorney.

Living Wills. Documents that are popularly called "living wills" may be notarized. These are not actually wills at all, but written statements of the signer's wishes concerning medical treatment in the event that person has an illness or injury and is unable to issue instructions on his or her own behalf.

MISCONDUCT, FINES AND PENALTIES

Misconduct

Misconduct Defined. "Official misconduct" generally takes place when a Washington Notary performs an act that is prohibited by law, or fails to perform an act that is required by law. The Notary's appointment is subject to revocation, suspension or denial by the Department of Licensing. (RCW 42.44.030 and 42.44.160)

Serious Crime Defined. A "serious crime" is defined as any felony or lesser crime that involves false swearing, misrepresentation, fraud, unauthorized practice of law, deceit, bribery, extortion, misappropriation, theft, conspiracy, interference with the administration of justice, or the solicitation of another to commit a crime. (RCW 42.44.010)

Qualification and Maintenance of Appointment

Cause for Denial. The Department of Licensing may deny a notarial appointment for the following reasons: (RCW 42.44.030)

- Conviction of a serious crime;

- Revocation, suspension or restriction of a Notary appointment or other professional license in Washington or any other state;

- Engaging in official misconduct, whether or not criminal penalties resulted; or

- Performance of a notarial act in a manner that would constitute negligence or disregard for the notarial office.

Revocation. The Department of Licensing may revoke a Notary's appointment for any one of the following reasons: (RCW 42.44.030 and 42.44.170)

- Conviction of a serious crime;

- Suspension or revocation of a professional license in Washington or any other state;

- Knowingly completing a false certificate;

- Performing a notarial act in a negligent manner; or

- Having been official adjudged "incompetent" by judicial finding.

Judgment of Incompetence by Judicial Finding. The Department of Licensing may revoke a Notary's appointment if the Notary is found incompetent by a court. In this case, the Notary's guardian or conservator must deliver a letter of resignation within 30 days of judgment to the Department of Licensing on behalf of the Notary. The letter must be accompanied by the Notary's seal or stamp. (RCW 42.44.170)

Failure to Maintain Commission Qualifications. A Notary who fails to maintain the qualifications of a Notary appointment (see

"How to Become a Washington Notary Public," page 3) is subject to commission revocation. (WAC 308-30-150)

Action on Other Professional License. A Notary applicant who had a professional license revoked, suspended, restricted or denied due to misconduct, dishonesty or similar causes is subject to having the Notary appointment revoked or denied. (RCW 42.44.030)

Conviction of Felony or Crime of Moral Turpitude. A Notary who is convicted of a felony or crime involving moral turpitude may have his or her appointment revoked, suspended or denied by the Department of Licensing. (RCW 42.44.030))

Must Report Conviction. Within 30 days of having been convicted of a felony or lesser offense — such as falsifying records, false swearing and giving false information, etc. — the Notary must file a written statement with the Department of Licensing. The statement must contain: the Notary's name, appointment number and appointment expiration date; the type of conviction and sentence; and the court and jurisdiction in which the Notary was convicted. Judgments against the Notary for any civil action should also be reported. (WAC 308-30-140)

Illegal and Improper Acts

Impersonating a Notary. A person who does not have a valid Notary appointment and who impersonates a Notary is guilty of a gross misdemeanor. (RCW 42.44.160)

Unauthorized Practice of Law. A Notary may not give legal advice or accept fees for legal advice. A nonattorney Notary is generally not permitted to assist other persons in drafting, preparing, completing or understanding a document or transaction. A Notary who engages in the unauthorized practice of law is guilty of a misdemeanor. (See "Unauthorized Practice of Law," page 54.) (RCW 2.48.170, 2.48.180 and WAC 308-30-090)

Notarize Own Signature. Notaries are not permitted to notarize their own signatures or documents in which they are named. (RCW 42.44.080)

False Certificate. In completing a false certificate — for

example, stating a signer appeared when he or she actually did not — a Notary may be guilty of a gross misdemeanor. (RCW 42.20.050 and 42.44.160)

Completing False Document. A Notary who falsely completes a document may be guilty of forgery with intent to deceive or defraud. Falsely completing a document is a Class C felony. (RCW 9A.60.020)

Failure to Require Personal Appearance. A Notary may not notarize any document without the signer personally appearing before the Notary. Since notarial certificate wording specifies that the signer appeared before the Notary at the time of notarization, failing to require such personal appearance may comprise completion of a false certificate, which is a gross misdemeanor. (42.20.050 and 42.44.160)

Endorsements and Testimonials. Notaries may not use their seals or the title "Notary Public" for any use except official notarial purposes. A Notary may not promote or endorse any product, service, contest, candidate or other offering. (WAC 308-30-160)

Overcharging. A Notary may not charge more than the maximum fees allowed by law. Charging more than the prescribed maximum fees is considered "requesting unlawful compensation" and is a Class C felony. (RCW 9A.68.020)

Fees Not Posted. A Notary must post the notarization fee schedule in a conspicuous area in no smaller than 10-point type. (WAC 308-30-020)

Copy or Notarize Naturalization Certificates. It can be a serious violation of federal law to make a typewritten, photostatic, or any other copy of a certificate of naturalization or notarize it. Severe penalties are prescribed, including imprisonment. (U.S. Penal Code, Sec. 75 and U.S. Code, Title 18, Sec. 137)

Signature Under Duress. No person, including a Notary, may force a person to sign an instrument. A person is guilty of obtaining a signature by deception or duress if by intention to deceive or defraud he or she causes the signer to execute an instrument. Such offense of a Class C felony. (RCW 9A.60.030)

Failure to Perform Duty. A public servant, such as a Notary, is guilty of official misconduct and a gross misdemeanor upon failure to fully and faithfully perform duties prescribed by law. (RCW 9A.80.010)

Duty Performed by Another for Profit. No public officer may willingly grant authority to, or accept a fee from, another person who intends to exercise the duties of that public office. (RCW 42.20.020)

Notarial Seal

Disposition of the Notary's Seal. Upon revocation or resignation of the Notary's commission, the Notary seal and/or stamp must be delivered to the Department of Licensing. (WAC 308-30-040)

When a Notary resigns the commission, the Notary seal and/or stamp must be filed with the Secretary of State at the same time the Notary files the letter of resignation. (WAC 308-30-040)

When a commission expires naturally after the four-year term, the Notary is not required to submit the seal or stamp to the Department of Licensing, but should destroy the seal or stamp as soon as possible to eliminate the chance of fraudulent misuse.

Should the Notary die during the commission term, the Notary's personal representative should destroy the seal or stamp. Any notarial records (e.g., the journal) should be retained for a reasonable amount of time, typically for the amount of time prescribed by the statute of limitations.

Unauthorized Manufacturing of Seal. It is unlawful to manufacture, give, sell, buy or possess a Notary seal or stamp if the Department of Licensing has not issued a Certificate of Appointment. Further, a Notary may not obtain a seal or stamp from a manufacturer without first presenting a photocopy of the Certificate of Appointment — or duplicate certificate in the case of a name change. (RCW 42.44.050 and WAC 308-30-010)

Seal Exclusive Property of Notary. A Notary's seal and stamp are the exclusive property of the Notary named on them. The seal and stamp may not be used by any other person or surrendered to an employer upon termination of employment. (RCW 42.44.090)

Investigation and Appeal

<u>Liable for All Damages</u>. A person injured by the misconduct or negligence of a Notary may sue to recover damages. A civil lawsuit against the Notary may seek financial recovery for the full extent of damages.

Notary errors and omissions insurance, however, provides protection for a Notary who is sued for damages resulting from *unintentional* mistakes made while performing notarial acts. Such insurance is optional and is available from many sources. Errors and omissions insurance does *not* cover the Notary for intentional misconduct.

<u>Denial of Appointment</u>. Should a Notary wish to appeal a denial or revocation of his or her Notary appointment, he or she must submit a notice in writing and mail or deliver it to the Department of Licensing. The written notice of appeal must be received by the Department within 20 days of the date of denial or revocation, or the applicant will lose the right to appeal. (WAC 308-30-080) ∎

Test Your Knowledge

Trial Exam

Instructions. This examination is designed to test your knowledge of the basic concepts of notarization. Work through the exam without looking at the answers, then check your responses and note where you need additional study. Careful review of "Notary Laws Explained" (pages 18–67), the reprinted Notary statutes (RCW) and Administrative Code regulations (WAC) (pages 74–104), "10 Most-Asked Questions" (pages 8–12) and "Steps to Proper Notarization" (pages 13–17) will produce the answers.

A perfect score on this examination is 100 points. There are:

- 20 true/false questions worth 1 point each
- 5 multiple-choice questions worth 4 points each
- 5 fill-in-the-blank questions worth 4 points each
- 5 essay questions worth 8 points each.

Now, get a separate sheet of paper and a pen or pencil, and get ready to test your knowledge.

Part 1: True/False. For the following statements, answer true or false. Each correct answer is worth 1 point:

1. Notaries may act only in the county where they are commissioned. True or false?

2. The maximum Notary fee for taking the acknowledgment of three signers is $15. True or false?

3. It is a Notary's duty to serve all persons requesting lawful

notarial acts, unless the Notary's employer has a policy otherwise. True or false?

4. Notaries must keep a photocopy of every document notarized. True or false?

5. A deposition is oral testimony that is written down and used as evidence in a court proceeding. True or false?

6. Notaries can withhold their services if they believe a signer is incoherent and unable to understand a document. True or false?

7. It is a Notary's duty to draft powers of attorney, mortgages, and deeds, upon request. True or false?

8. The letters "L.S." stand for the Latin words *locus sigilli*, which mean "location of the seal." True or false?

9. Holographic wills must be notarized to be valid. True or false?

10. A credible witness vouches for the identity of a signer in the Notary's presence. True or false?

11. Notaries may notarize documents executed by the company that employs them. True or false?

12. A Notary who does not charge fees is not required to post a fee schedule. True or false?

13. The Notary needn't reimburse the insurance company for E&O insurance funds paid out to a person financially harmed by the Notary's actions. True or false?

14. A Notary is not required to verify that a sworn signer has the authority to sign as a corporate officer. True or false?

15. A Notary's seal and journal belong to the Notary's employer if the employer paid for them. True or false?

16. An acknowledgment certificate is not to be used for jurats. True or false?

17. An affirmation is the legal equivalent of an oath, but has no reference to a Supreme Being. True or false?

18. If presented with a document that does not include notarial wording, the Notary should automatically attach and complete an acknowledgment. True or false?

19. Notaries may not refuse to notarize blank or incomplete documents if they are signed in the Notary's presence. True or false?

20. A Notary may notarize a deed in which the Notary is named. True or false?

<u>Multiple Choice</u>. Choose the one best answer to each question. Each correct answer is worth 4 points.

1. A Notary has a disqualifying interest when acting as...
    a. A legal secretary typing papers under the instruction of an employer-attorney for a client.
    b. A bank employee preparing loan documents.
    c. A real estate agent selling a condominium and getting a commission.

2. To become a Notary, an applicant must...
    a. Have been a state resident for at least one year.
    b. Be at least 18 years old.
    c. Pass an oral exam given by the governor's office.

3. A certificate of authority for a Notary may be obtained...
    a. From the Governor's office or the County Clerk.
    b. From a stationery store or the Notary himself/herself.
    c. From the Department of Licensing.

4. "Satisfactory evidence" of identity means reliance on...
    a. ID cards only.
    b. Personal knowledge of identity only.
    c. A credible witness or ID cards.

5. A Washington Notary may...
    a. Take verifications under oath or affirmation.
    b. Correct errors in the document being notarized.

TEST YOUR KNOWLEDGE

c. Certify a copy of a foreign birth certificate.

<u>Fill in the Blank</u>. Write in the word or phrase that best completes each sentence. Each correct answer is worth 4 points.

1. The Notary and the Notary's _____ are liable for the Notary's unintentional mistakes.

2. A solemn, spoken pledge that is not an affirmation is called an _____.

3. An acceptable ID card should contain a signature, physical description and _____ of its bearer.

4. A certified copy certifies the _____ of the reproduction.

5. Wills written entirely in the testator's own handwriting are called _____.

<u>Essay</u>. Reply to each question or statement with a short paragraph. Each complete and correct response is worth 8 points.

1. Discuss the reasons to obtain Notary errors and omissions insurance.

2. How does a proof of acknowledgment by subscribing witness work?

3. What is an *apostille* and when is it used?

4. Why should a Notary always complete the journal entry before filling out a notarial certificate?

5. Outline the differences between an acknowledgment certificate and a jurat.

Test Answers

<u>True/False</u>. 1. F; 2. F; 3. F; 4. F; 5. T; 6. T; 7. F; 8. T; 9. F; 10. T; 11. T; 12. T; 13. T; 14. T; 15. F; 16. T; 17. T; 18. F; 19. F; 20. F

<u>Multiple Choice</u>. 1. c; 2. b; 3. c; 4. c; 5. a

WASHINGTON NOTARY LAW PRIMER

<u>Fill in the Blank</u>. 1. E&O insurer 2. Oath; 3. Photograph; 4. Accuracy; 5. Holographic

<u>Essay</u>. Responses should include the basic information in the paragraphs below:

1. Notary errors and omissions insurance protects Notaries from actions against them for unintentional errors. Purchased from a state-licensed company, Notary errors and omissions insurance protects the Notary in case of such an unintentional error, but only up to the policy limit. The Notary is not required to reimburse the insurance company.

2. A proof of acknowledgment in lieu of an acknowledgment is sometimes used when a real estate document's principal signer is unavailable to appear before a Notary. In most such cases, the principal will be out of town, out of state or even out of the country. A subscribing witness who has either seen the principal sign the document or taken the principal's acknowledgment of the signature may present this document to a Notary on the principal's behalf. The witness must sign (subscribe) the document in addition to the principal. The witness, who must be personally known to the Notary, is given an oath by the Notary. A person who is a grantee or beneficiary of a document should not serve as a subscribing witness.

3. An *apostille* is a certificate authenticating the signature and seal/stamp of a Notary. It is issued under provisions of an international treaty, signed by more than 50 nations, called the Hague Convention Abolishing the Requirement of Legalization for Foreign Public Documents. For notarized documents exchanged between the subscribing nations, this treaty streamlines the time-consuming authentication process known as "chain certification" by requiring only one authenticating certificate, the *apostille* (French for "notation"). *Apostilles* for Washington Notaries are issued by the Department of State's Business & Occupations Unit.

4. Filling out a journal entry before completing a notarial certificate prevents a signer from grabbing the document and leaving before an important record of the notarization is

made in the journal.

5. An acknowledgment certificate certifies that the signer of the document personally appeared before the Notary on the date and in the county indicated. It also certifies that the signer's identity was satisfactorily proven to the Notary and that the signer acknowledged having signed freely. A jurat certifies that the person signing the document did so in the Notary's presence, that the person appeared before the Notary on the date and in the county indicated, and that the Notary administered an oath or affirmation to the signer. For a jurat, it is also required that the Notary positively identify the signer.

Tally Your Score

After checking your answers, add up your score. Then look at the grading scale below to determine how you stand:

- 90–100: Excellent!
- 80–89: Good, but some review needed.
- 70–79: Fair. Reread the parts of the *Primer* covering the answers you missed.
- Below 70: Below par. Study the laws thoroughly again. ■

Washington Laws Pertaining to Notaries Public

Reprinted on the following pages is the complete text of the enacted laws and administrative regulations affecting Notaries and notarial acts, drawn from the Revised Code of Washington (RCW) and the Washington Administrative Code (WAC). Citations in brackets at the end of each section indicate the legislative history of the section.

Revised Code of Washington
CHAPTER 42.44 RCW
NOTARIES PUBLIC

Sections
42.44.010	Definitions.
42.44.020	Qualifications—Application—Bond.
42.44.030	Appointment denied certain persons.
42.44.040	Certificate of appointment.
42.44.050	Seal or stamp.
42.44.060	Term.
42.44.070	Reappointment without endorsements.
42.44.080	Standards for notarial acts.
42.44.090	Form of certificate—General—Seal or stamp as exclusive property.
42.44.100	Short forms of certificate.
42.44.110	Illegible writing.
42.44.120	Fees.
42.44.130	Notarial acts by officials of other jurisdictions.
42.44.140	Notarial acts by federal authorities.
42.44.150	Notarial acts by foreign authorities.
42.44.160	Official misconduct—Penalty.
42.44.170	Revocation of appointment—Resignation.
42.44.180	Evidence of authenticity of notarial seal and signature.

WASHINGTON LAWS PERTAINING TO NOTARIES PUBLIC

42.44.190 Rules.
42.44.200 Transfer of records.
42.44.900 Savings—1985 c 156.
42.44.901 Construction.
42.44.902 Severability—1985 c 156.
42.44.903 Effective date—1985 c 156.

RCW 42.44.010 Definitions. Unless the context clearly requires otherwise, the definitions in this section apply throughout this chapter.

(1) "Director" means the director of licensing of the state of Washington or the director's designee.

(2) "Notarial act" and "notarization" mean:
(a) Taking an acknowledgment;
(b) administering an oath or affirmation;
(c) taking a verification upon oath or affirmation;
(d) witnessing or attesting a signature;
(e) certifying or attesting a copy;
(f) receiving a protest of a negotiable instrument;
(g) certifying that an event has occurred or an act has been performed; and
(h) any other act that a notary public of this state is authorized to perform.

(3) "Notary public" and "notary" mean any person appointed to perform notarial acts in this state.

(4) "Acknowledgment" means a statement by a person that the person has executed an instrument as the person's free and voluntary act for the uses and purposes stated therein and, if the instrument is executed in a representative capacity, a statement that the person signed the document with proper authority and executed it as the act of the person or entity represented and identified therein.

(5) "Verification upon oath or affirmation" means a statement by a person who asserts it to be true and makes the assertion upon oath or affirmation administered in accordance with chapter 5.28 RCW.

(6) "In a representative capacity" means:
(a) For and on behalf of a corporation, partnership, trust, or other entity, as an authorized officer, agent, partner, trustee, or other representative;
(b) As a public officer, personal representative, guardian, or other representative, in the capacity recited in the instrument;
(c) As an attorney in fact for a principal; or
(d) In any other capacity as an authorized representative of another.

(7) "Serious crime" means any felony or any lesser crime, a necessary element of which, as determined by the statutory or common law definition of such crime, involves interference with the administration of justice, false swearing, misrepresentation, fraud, the unauthorized practice of law, deceit, bribery, extortion, misappropriation, theft, or an attempt, a conspiracy, or the solicitation of another to commit a serious crime. [1985 c 156 §1.]

RCW 42.44.020 Qualifications—Application—Bond. (1) The director may, upon application, appoint to be a notary public in this state, any person who:
(a) Is at least eighteen years of age;
(b) Resides in Washington state, or resides in an adjoining state and is regularly employed in Washington state or carries on business in Washington

state; and
(c) Can read and write English.

(2) Each application shall be accompanied by endorsements by at least three residents of this state of the age of eighteen or more, who are not relatives of the applicant, in the following form:

> I, (name of endorser), being a person eligible to vote in the state of Washington, believe the applicant for a notary public appointment, (applicant's name), who is not related to me, to be a person of integrity and good moral character and capable of performing notarial acts.
> _____ (Endorser's signature and address, with date of signing)

(3) Every application for appointment as a notary public shall be accompanied by a fee established by the director by rule.

(4) Every applicant for appointment as a notary public shall submit an application in a form prescribed by the director, and shall sign the following declaration in the presence of a notary public of this state:

> Declaration of Applicant
> I, (name of applicant), solemnly swear or affirm under penalty of perjury that the personal information I have provided in this application is true, complete, and correct; that I carefully have read the materials provided with the application describing the duties of a notary public in and for the state of Washington; and, that I will perform, to the best of my ability, all notarial acts in accordance with the law.
> _____ (Signature of applicant)

> State of Washington
> County of _____
> On this day _____ appeared before me, signed this Declaration of Application, and swore (or affirmed) that (he/she) understood its contents and that its contents are truthful.
> Dated: _____
> _____ Signature of notary public   (Seal or stamp)
> Residing at _____

(5) Every applicant shall submit to the director proof from a surety company that a ten thousand dollar surety bond, insuring the proper performance of notarial acts by the applicant, will be effective for a term commencing on the date the person is appointed, and expiring on the date the applicant's notary appointment expires. The surety for the bond shall be a company qualified to write surety bonds in this state. [1985 c 156 §2.]

RCW 42.44.030 Appointment denied certain persons. The director may deny appointment as a notary public to any person who:
(1) Has been convicted of a serious crime;
(2) Has had a notary appointment or other professional license revoked, suspended, or restricted in this or any other state;
(3) Has engaged in official misconduct as defined in *section17(1) of this act, whether or not criminal penalties resulted; or

WASHINGTON LAWS PERTAINING TO NOTARIES PUBLIC

(4) Has performed a notarial act or acts in a manner found by the director to constitute gross negligence, a course of negligent conduct, or reckless disregard of his or her responsibility as a notary public. [1985 c 156 §3.]

Reviser's note: A literal translation of "section 17(1) of this act" would be RCW 42.44.170(1); however, RCW 42.44.160(1) was apparently intended.

RCW 42.44.040 Certificate of appointment. The director shall deliver a certificate evidencing the appointment to each person appointed as a notary public. The certificate may be signed in facsimile by the governor, the secretary of state, and the director or the director's designee. The certificate shall bear a printed seal of the state of Washington. [1985 c 156 §4.]

RCW 42.44.050 Seal or stamp. Every person appointed as a notary public in this state shall procure a seal or stamp, on which shall be engraved or impressed the words "Notary Public" and "State of Washington," the date the appointment expires, the person's surname, and at least the initials of the person's first and middle names. The director shall prescribe by rule the size and form or forms of the seal or stamp. It is unlawful for any person intentionally to manufacture, give, sell, procure or possess a seal or stamp evidencing the current appointment of a person as a notary public until the director has delivered a certificate evidencing the appointment as provided for in RCW 42.44.040. [1985 c 156 §5.]

RCW 42.44.060 Term. A person appointed as a notary public by the director may perform notarial acts in this state for a term of four years, unless:

(1) The notarial appointment has been revoked under RCW 42.44.130 or 42.44.140; or

(2) The notarial appointment has been resigned. [1985 c 156 §6.]

RCW 42.44.070 Reappointment without endorsements. A person who has received an appointment as a notary public may be reappointed without the endorsements required in RCW 42.44.020(2) if the person submits a new application before the expiration date of the current appointment. [1985 c 156 §7.]

RCW 42.44.080 Standards for notarial acts. A notary public is authorized to perform notarial acts in this state. Notarial acts shall be performed in accordance with the following, as applicable:

(1) In taking an acknowledgment, a notary public must determine and certify, either from personal knowledge or from satisfactory evidence, that the person appearing before the notary public and making the acknowledgement is the person whose true signature is on the document.

(2) In taking an acknowledgment authorized by RCW 64.08.100 from a person physically unable to sign his or her name or make a mark, a notary public shall, in addition to other requirements for taking an acknowledgment, determine and certify from personal knowledge or satisfactory evidence that the person appearing before the notary public is physically unable to sign his or her name or make a mark and is otherwise competent. The notary public shall include in the acknowledgment a statement that the signature in the acknowledgment was obtained under the authority of RCW 64.08.100.

(3) In taking a verification upon oath or affirmation, a notary public must

WASHINGTON NOTARY LAW PRIMER

determine, either from personal knowledge or from satisfactory evidence, that the person appearing before the notary public and making the verification is the person whose true signature is on the statement verified.

(4) In witnessing or attesting a signature, a notary public must determine, either from personal knowledge or from satisfactory evidence, that the signature is that of the person appearing before the notary public and named in the document.

(5) In certifying or attesting a copy of a document or other item, a notary public must determine that the proffered copy is a full, true, and accurate transcription or reproduction of that which was copied.

(6) In making or noting a protest of a negotiable instrument, a notary public must determine the matters set forth in *RCW 62A.3-509.

(7) In certifying that an event has occurred or an act has been performed, a notary public must determine the occurrence or performance either from personal knowledge or from satisfactory evidence based upon the oath or affirmation of a credible witness personally known to the notary public.

(8) A notary public has satisfactory evidence that a person is the person described in a document if that person: (a) Is personally known to the notary public; (b) is identified upon the oath or affirmation of a credible witness personally known to the notary public; or (c) is identified on the basis of identification documents.

(9) The signature and seal or stamp of a notary public are prima facie evidence that the signature of the notary is genuine and that the person is a notary public.

(10) A notary public is disqualified from performing a notarial act when the notary is a signer of the document which is to be notarized. [1987 c 76 §3; 1985 c 156 §8.]

*Reviser's note: RCW 62A.3-509 was repealed by 1993 c 229 §76, effective July 1, 1994.

RCW 42.44.090 Form of certificate—General—Seal or stamp as exclusive property. (1) A notarial act by a notary public must be evidenced by a certificate signed and dated by a notary public. The certificate must include the name of the jurisdiction in which the notarial act is performed and the title of the notary public or other notarial officer and shall be accompanied by an impression of the official seal or stamp. It shall not be necessary for a notary public in certifying an oath to be used in any of the courts in this state, to append an impression of the official seal or stamp. If the notarial officer is a notary public, the certificate shall also indicate the date of expiration of such notary public's appointment, but omission of that information may subsequently be corrected.

(2) A certificate of a notarial act is sufficient if it meets the requirements of subsection (1) of this section and it:

(a) Is in the short form set forth in RCW 42.44.100;

(b) Is in a form otherwise permitted or prescribed by the laws of this state;

(c) Is in a form prescribed by the laws or regulations applicable in the place in which the notarial act was performed; or

(d) Is in a form that sets forth the actions of the notary public and the described actions are sufficient to meet the requirements of the designated notarial act.

If any law of this state specifically requires a certificate in a form other than that set forth in RCW 42.44.100 in connection with a form of document or transaction, the certificate required by such law shall be used for such document or transaction.

(3) By executing a certificate of a notarial act, the notary public certifies that he or she has made the determinations required by RCW 42.44.080.

(4) A notary public's seal or stamp shall be the exclusive property of the notary public, shall not be used by any other person, and shall not be surrendered to an employer upon termination of employment, regardless of whether the employer paid for the seal or for the notary's bond or appointment fees. [1985c 156 §9.]

RCW 42.44.100 Short forms of certificate. The following short forms of notarial certificates are sufficient for the purposes indicated, if completed with the information required by this section:

(1) For an acknowledgment in an individual capacity:

State of Washington
County of _____
    I certify that I know or have satisfactory evidence that (name of person) is the person who appeared before me, and said person acknowledged that (he/she) signed this instrument and acknowledged it to be (his/her) free and voluntary act for the uses and purposes mentioned in the instrument.
Dated: _____
(Signature)   (Seal or stamp)
Title _____
My appointment expires _____

(2) For an acknowledgment in a representative capacity:

State of Washington
County of _____
    I certify that I know or have satisfactory evidence that (name of person) is the person who appeared before me, and said person acknowledged that (he/she) signed this instrument, on oath stated that (he/she) was authorized to execute the instrument and acknowledged it as the (type of authority, e.g., officer, trustee, etc.) of (name of party on behalf of whom instrument was executed) to be the free and voluntary act of such party for the uses and purposes mentioned in the instrument.
Dated: _____
(Signature)   (Seal or stamp)
Title _____
My appointment expires _____

(3) For a verification upon oath or affirmation:

State of Washington
County of _____
    Signed and sworn to (or affirmed) before me on (date) by (name

of person making statement).
(Signature)   (Seal or stamp)
Title _____
My appointment expires _____

(4) For witnessing or attesting a signature:

State of Washington
County of _____
    Signed or attested before me on _____ by _____.
(Signature)   (Seal or stamp)
Title _____
My appointment expires _____

(5) For attestation of a copy of a document:

State of Washington
County of _____
    I certify that this is a true and correct copy of a document in the possession of _____ as of this date.
Dated: _____
(Signature)   (Seal or stamp)
Title _____
My appointment expires _____

(6) For certifying the occurrence of an event or the performance of an act:

State of Washington
County of _____
    I certify that the event or act described in this document has occurred or been performed.
Dated: _____
(Signature)   (Seal or stamp)
Title _____
My appointment expires _____

[1988 c 69 §4; 1985 c 156 §10.]

RCW 42.44.110 Illegible writing. The illegibility of any wording, writing, or marking required under this chapter does not in and of itself affect the validity of a document or transaction. [1985 c 156 §11.]

RCW 42.44.120 Fees. (1) The director shall establish by rule the maximum fees that may be charged by notaries public for various notarial services.
(2) A notary public need not charge fees for notarial acts. [1985 c 156 §12.]

RCW 42.44.130 Notarial acts by officials of other jurisdictions. (1) A notarial act has the same effect under the law of this state as if performed by a notary public of this state, if performed in another state, commonwealth, territory, district, or possession of the United States by any of the following persons:
    (a) A notary public of that jurisdiction;
    (b) A judge, clerk, or deputy clerk of a court of that jurisdiction; or

(c) Any other person authorized by the law of that jurisdiction to perform notarial acts.

Notarial acts performed in other jurisdictions of the United States under federal authority as provided in RCW 42.44.140 have the same effect as if performed by a notarial officer of this state.

(2) The signature and title of a person performing a notarial act are prima facie evidence that the signature is genuine and that the person holds the designated title.

(3) The signature and title of an officer listed in subsection (1) (a) and (b) of this section conclusively establish the authority of a holder of that title to perform a notarial act. [1985 c 156 §13.]

RCW 42.44.140 Notarial acts by federal authorities. (1) A notarial act has the same effect under the law of this state as if performed by a notary public of this state if performed by any of the following persons under authority granted by the law of the United States:

(a) A judge, clerk, or deputy clerk of a court;

(b) A commissioned officer in active service with the military forces of the United States;

(c) An officer of the foreign service or consular agent of the United States; or

(d) Any other person authorized by federal law to perform notarial acts.

(2) The signature and title of a person performing a notarial act are prima facie evidence that the signature is genuine and that the person holds the designated title.

(3) The signature and title or rank of an officer listed in subsection (1) (a), (b), and (c) of this section conclusively establish the authority of a holder of that title to perform a notarial act. [1985 c 156 §14.]

RCW 42.44.150 Notarial acts by foreign authorities. (1) A notarial act has the same effect under the law of this state as if performed by a notary public of this state if performed within the jurisdiction of and under authority of a foreign nation or its constituent units or a multinational or international organization by any of the following persons:

(a) A notary public or notary;

(b) A judge, clerk, or deputy clerk of a court of record; or

(c) Any other person authorized by the law of that jurisdiction to perform notarial acts.

(2) An "apostille" in the form prescribed by the Hague Convention of October 5, 1961, conclusively establishes that the signature of the notarial officer is genuine and that the officer holds the designated office.

(3) A certificate by a foreign service or consular officer of the United States stationed in the nation under the jurisdiction of which the notarial act was performed, or a certificate by a foreign service or consular officer of that nation stationed in the United States, is prima facie evidence of the authenticity or validity of the notarial act set forth in the certificate.

(4) A stamp or seal of the person performing the notarial act is prima facie evidence that the signature is genuine and that the person holds that designated title.

(5) A stamp or seal of an officer listed in subsection (1) (a) or (b) of this section is prima facie evidence that a person with that title has authority to

perform notarial acts.

(6) If the title of officer and indication of authority to perform notarial acts appears either in a digest of foreign law or in a list customarily used as a source for that information, the authority of an officer with that title to perform notarial acts is conclusively established. [1985 c 156 §15.]

RCW 42.44.160 Official misconduct—Penalty. (1) A notary public commits official misconduct when he or she signs a certificate evidencing a notarial act, knowing that the contents of the certificate are false.

(2) A notary public who commits an act of official misconduct shall be guilty of a gross misdemeanor.

(3) Any person not appointed as a notary public who acts as or otherwise impersonates a notary public shall be guilty of a gross misdemeanor. [1985 c 156 §16.]

RCW 42.44.170 Revocation of appointment—Resignation. (1) The director may revoke the appointment of any notary public for any reason for which appointment may be denied under RCW 42.44.030.

(2) The director shall revoke the appointment of a notary public upon a judicial finding of incompetency of the notary public. If a notary public is found to be incompetent, his or her guardian or conservator shall within thirty days of such finding mail or deliver to the director a letter of resignation on behalf of the notary public.

(3) A notary public may voluntarily resign by mailing or delivering to the director a letter of resignation. [1985 c 156 §17.]

RCW 42.44.180 Evidence of authenticity of notarial seal and signature. (1) The authenticity of the notarial seal and official signature of a notary public of this state may be evidenced by:

(a) A certificate of authority from the director or the secretary of state; or

(b) An apostille in the form prescribed by the Hague Convention Abolishing the Requirement of Legalization for Foreign Public Documents of October 5, 1961.

(2) An apostille as specified by the Hague Convention shall be attached to any document requiring authentication that is sent to a nation that has signed and ratified the Hague Convention Abolishing the Requirement of Legalization for Foreign Public Documents. [1985 c 156 §18.]

RCW 42.44.190 Rules. On or before January 1, 1986, the director shall adopt rules to carry out this chapter. Such rules shall include but shall not be limited to rules concerning applications for appointment, application and renewal fees, fees chargeable for notarial services, the replacement of lost or stolen seals or stamps, changes of names or addresses of notaries, resignations of notaries, appeals of denials and revocations of appointments, and issuance of evidences of authenticity of notarial seals and signatures. [1985 c 156 §20.]

RCW 42.44.200 Transfer of records. Records relating to the appointment and commissioning of notaries public that are in the custody of county clerks of this state on *the effective date of this act shall be transferred to the director of licensing on or before December 31, 1985. Such records may be archived by the director. [1985 c 156 §22.]

Reviser's note: As used in this section, the phrase "the effective date of this act," is ambiguous; see RCW 42.44.903.

RCW 42.44.900 Savings—1985 c 156. Nothing in *this act may be interpreted to revoke any notary public appointment or commission existing on January 1, 1986. *This act does not terminate, or in any way modify, any liability, civil or criminal, which exists on January 1, 1986. A notarial act performed before January 1, 1986, is not affected by *this act. [1985 c 156 §21.]

Reviser's note: "This act" [1985 c 156] consisted of the enactment of RCW 42.44.010 through 42.44.200 and 42.44.900 through 42.44.903, the amendment of RCW 43.07.035, and the repeal of chapter 42.28 RCW and RCW 43.06.100, 43.131.299, and 43.131.300.

RCW 42.44.901 Construction. RCW 42.44.010, 42.44.080, 42.44.090, 42.44.100, 42.44.130, 42.44.140, and 42.44.150 shall be applied and construed to effectuate their general purpose to make the law uniform with respect to the subject of this chapter among states enacting such sections of this chapter. [1985 c 156 §23.]

RCW 42.44.902 Severability—1985 c 156. If any provision of this act or its application to any person or circumstance is held invalid, the remainder of the act or the application of the provision to other persons or circumstances is not affected. [1985c 156 §24.]

RCW 42.44.903 Effective date—1985 c 156. Sections 1 through 19, 21, and 23 through 26 shall take effect on January 1, 1986. [1985 c 156 §27.]

Reviser's note: For translation of above references see Codification Tables, Volume 0.

Additional Pertinent Statutes

TITLE 2. COURTS OF RECORD
Chapter 2.48 State bar act.

RCW 2.48.170 Only active members may practice law. No person shall practice law in this state subsequent to the first meeting of the state bar unless he shall be an active member thereof as hereinbefore defined: PROVIDED, That a member of the bar in good standing in any other state or jurisdiction shall be entitled to appear in the courts of this state under such rules as the board of governors may prescribe. [1933 c 94 §13; RRS §138-13.]

NOTES: Rules of court: Admission—APR 5.

RCW 2.48.180 Definitions—Unlawful practice a crime—Cause for discipline—Unprofessional conduct—Defense—Injunction—Remedies—Costs—Attorneys' fees—Time limit for action.
(1) As used in this section:
(a) "Legal provider" means an active member in good standing of the state bar, and any other person authorized by the Washington state supreme court to

engage in full or limited practice of law;

(b) "Nonlawyer" means a person to whom the Washington supreme court has granted a limited authorization to practice law but who practices law outside that authorization, and a person who is not an active member in good standing of the state bar, including persons who are disbarred or suspended from membership;

(c) "Ownership interest" means the right to control the affairs of a business, or the right to share in the profits of a business, and includes a loan to the business when the interest on the loan is based upon the income of the business or the loan carries more than a commercially reasonable rate of interest.

(2) The following constitutes unlawful practice of law:

(a) A nonlawyer practices law, or holds himself or herself out as entitled to practice law;

(b) A legal provider holds an investment or ownership interest in a business primarily engaged in the practice of law, knowing that a nonlawyer holds an investment or ownership interest in the business;

(c) A nonlawyer knowingly holds an investment or ownership interest in a business primarily engaged in the practice of law;

(d) A legal provider works for a business that is primarily engaged in the practice of law, knowing that a nonlawyer holds an investment or ownership interest in the business; or

(e) A nonlawyer shares legal fees with a legal provider.

(3) Unlawful practice of law is a crime. A single violation of this section is a gross misdemeanor. Each subsequent violation, whether alleged in the same or in subsequent prosecutions, is a class C felony.

(4) Nothing contained in this section affects the power of the courts to grant injunctive or other equitable relief or to punish as for contempt.

(5) Whenever a legal provider or a person licensed by the state in a business or profession is convicted, enjoined, or found liable for damages or a civil penalty or other equitable relief under this section, the plaintiff's attorney shall provide written notification of the judgment to the appropriate regulatory or disciplinary body or agency.

(6) A violation of this section is cause for discipline and constitutes unprofessional conduct that could result in any regulatory penalty provided by law, including refusal, revocation,or suspension of a business or professional license, or right or admission to practice. Conduct that constitutes a violation of this section is unprofessional conduct in violation of RCW18.130.180.

(7) In a proceeding under this section it is a defense if proven by the defendant by a preponderance of the evidence that, at the time of the offense, the conduct alleged was authorized by the rules of professional conduct or the admission to practice rules, or Washington business and professions licensing statutes or rules.

(8) Independent of authority granted to the attorney general, the prosecuting attorney may petition the superior court for an injunction against a person who has violated this chapter. Remedies in an injunctive action brought by a prosecuting attorney are limited to an order enjoining, restraining, or preventing the doing of any act or practice that constitutes a violation of this chapter and imposing a civil penalty of up to five thousand dollars for each violation. The prevailing party in the action may, in the discretion of the court, recover its reasonable investigative costs and the costs of the action including a reasonable attorney's fee. The degree of proof required in an action brought under this

subsection is a preponderance of the evidence. An action under this subsection must be brought within three years after the violation of this chapter occurred. [1995 c 285 §26; 1989 c 117 §13; 1933 c 94 §14; RRS §138-14.]

NOTES:Rules of court: RLD 1.1(h). Effective date—1995 c 285: See RCW 48.30A.900. Severability—Effective date—1989 c 117: See RCW 19.154.901 and 19.154.902. Practicing law with disbarred attorney: RCW 2.48.220(9).

TITLE 5. EVIDENCE
Chapter 5.28 Oaths and affirmations.

RCW 5.28.010 Who may administer. Every court, judge, clerk of a court, or notary public, is authorized to take testimony in any action, suit or proceeding, and such other persons in particular cases as authorized by law. Every such court or officer is authorized to collect fees established under RCW 36.18.020 and 36.18.012 through 36.18.018 and to administer oaths and affirmations generally and to every such other person in such particular case as authorized. [1995 c 292 § 1; 1987 c 202 § 124; 2 H. C. § 1693; 1869 p 378 § 1; RRS § 1264.]

RCW 5.28.020 How administered. An oath may be administered as follows: The person who swears holds up his hand, while the person administering the oath thus addresses him: "You do solemnly swear that the evidence you shall give in the issue (or matter) now pending between _____ and _____ shall be the truth, the whole truth, and nothing but the truth, so help you God." If the oath be administered to any other than a witness giving testimony, the form may be changed to: "You do solemnly swear you will true answers make to such questions as you may be asked," etc. [2 H. C. §1694; 1869 p 378 §2; RRS §1265.]

RCW 5.28.030 Form may be varied. Whenever the court or officer before which a person is offered as a witness is satisfied that he has a peculiar mode of swearing connected with or in addition to the usual form of administration, which, in witness' opinion, is more solemn or obligatory, the court or officer may, in its discretion, adopt that mode. [2 H. C. §1695; 1869 p 379 §3; RRS §1266.]

RCW 5.28.040 Form may be adapted to religious belief. When a person is sworn who believes in any other than the Christian religion, he may be sworn according to the peculiar ceremonies of his religion, if there be any such. [2 H. C. §1696; 1869 p 379 §4; RRS §1267.]

RCW 5.28.050 Form of affirmation. Any person who has conscientious scruples against taking an oath, may make his solemn affirmation, by assenting, when addressed, in the following manner: "You do solemnly affirm that," etc., as in RCW 5.28.020. [2 H. C.§1697; 1869 p 379 §5; RRS §1268.]

RCW 5.28.060 Affirmation equivalent to oath. Whenever an oath is required, an affirmation, as prescribed in RCW 5.28.050 is to be deemed equivalent thereto, and a false affirmation is to be deemed perjury, equally with a false oath. [2 H. C. §1698; 1869p 379 §6; RRS §1269.]

Chapter 5.52 Telegraphic communications.

RCW 5.52.050 Telegraphic copies as evidence. Except as hereinbefore otherwise provided, any instrument in writing, duly certified, under his hand and official seal, by a notary public, commissioner of deeds, or clerk of a court of record, to be genuine, within the personal knowledge of such officer, may, together with such certificate, be sent by telegraph and the telegraphic copy thereof shall, prima facie, only have the same force, effect and validity, in all respects whatsoever as the original, and the burden of proof shall rest with the party denying the genuineness, or due execution of the original. [Code 1881 § 2356; 1865 p 75 § 15; RRS § 11349.]

TITLE 9A. WASHINGTON CRIMINAL CODE
Chapter 9A.60 Fraud.

RCW 9A.60.010 Definitions. The following definitions and the definitions of RCW 9A.56.010 are applicable in this chapter unless the context otherwise requires:

(1) "Written instrument" means: (a) Any paper, document, or other instrument containing written or printed matter or its equivalent; or (b) any access device, as defined in RCW 9A.56.010(3), token, stamp, seal, badge, trademark, or other evidence or symbol of value, right, privilege, or identification;

(2) "Complete written instrument" means one which is fully drawn with respect to every essential feature thereof;

(3) "Incomplete written instrument" means one which contains some matter by way of content or authentication but which requires additional matter in order to render it a complete written instrument;

(4) To "falsely make" a written instrument means to make or draw a complete or incomplete written instrument which purports to be authentic, but which is not authentic either because the ostensible maker is fictitious or because, if real, he did not authorize the making or drawing thereof;

(5) To "falsely complete" a written instrument means to transform an incomplete written instrument into a complete one by adding or inserting matter, without the authority of anyone entitled to grant it;

(6) To "falsely alter" a written instrument means to change, without authorization by anyone entitled to grant it, a written instrument, whether complete or incomplete, by means of erasure, obliteration, deletion, insertion of new matter, transposition of matter, or in any other manner;

(7) "Forged instrument" means a written instrument which has been falsely made, completed or altered. [1987 c 140 §5; 1975-'762nd ex.s. c 38 §12; 1975 1st ex.s. c 260 §9A.60.010.]

RCW 9A.60.020 Forgery. (1) A person is guilty of forgery if, with intent to injure or defraud:

(a) He falsely makes, completes, or alters a written instrument or;

(b) He possesses, utters, offers, disposes of, or puts off as true a written instrument which he knows to be forged.

(2) Forgery is a class C felony. [1975-'76 2nd ex.s. c 38 §13; 1975 1st ex.s. c 260 §9A.60.020.]

RCW 9A.60.030 Obtaining a signature by deception or duress. (1) A person is guilty of obtaining a signature by deception or duress if by deception or duress and with intent to defraud or deprive he causes another person to sign or execute a written instrument.

(2) Obtaining a signature by deception or duress is a class C felony. [1975-'76 2nd ex.s. c 38 §14; 1975 1st ex.s. c 260 §9A.60.030.]

RCW 9A.60.040 Criminal impersonation. (1) A person is guilty of criminal impersonation in the first degree if the person:

(a) Assumes a false identity and does an act in his or her assumed character with intent to defraud another or for any other unlawful purpose; or

(b) Pretends to be a representative of some person or organization or a public servant and does an act in his or her pretended capacity with intent to defraud another or for any other unlawful purpose.

(2) Criminal impersonation in the first degree is a gross misdemeanor.

(3) A person is guilty of criminal impersonation in the second degree if the person:

(a) Claims to be a law enforcement officer or creates an impression that he or she is a law enforcement officer; and

(b) Under circumstances not amounting to criminal impersonation in the first degree, does an act with intent to convey the impression that he or she is acting in an official capacity and a reasonable person would believe the person is a law enforcement officer.

(4) Criminal impersonation in the second degree is a misdemeanor. [1993 c 457 §1; 1975 1st ex.s. c 260 §9A.60.040.]

RCW 9A.60.050 False certification. (1) A person is guilty of false certification, if, being an officer authorized to take a proof or acknowledgment of an instrument which by law may be recorded, he knowingly certifies falsely that the execution of such instrument was acknowledged by any party thereto or that the execution thereof was proved.

(2) False certification is a gross misdemeanor. [1975-'76 2nd ex.s. c 38 §15; 1975 1st ex.s. c 260 §9A.60.050.]

Chapter 9A.68 Bribery and corrupt influence.

RCW 9A.68.020 Requesting unlawful compensation. (1) A public servant is guilty of requesting unlawful compensation if he requests a pecuniary benefit for the performance of an official action knowing that he is required to perform that action without compensation or at a level of compensation lower than that requested.

(2) Requesting unlawful compensation is a class C felony. [1975 1st ex.s. c 260 §9A.68.020.]

Chapter 9A.80 Abuse of office.

RCW 9A.80.010 Official misconduct. (1) A public servant is guilty of official misconduct if, with intent to obtain a benefit or to deprive another person of a lawful right or privilege:

(a) He intentionally commits an unauthorized act under color of law; or
(b) He intentionally refrains from performing a duty imposed upon him by law.

(2) Official misconduct is a gross misdemeanor. [1975-'76 2nd ex.s. c 38 §17; 1975 1st ex.s. c 260 §9A.80.010.]

TITLE 26. DOMESTIC RELATIONS
Chapter 26.04 Marriage.

RCW 26.04.150 Application for license—May be secured by mail—Execution and acknowledgment. Any person may secure by mail from the county auditor of the county in the state of Washington where he intends to be married, an application, and execute and acknowledge said application before a notary public. [1963 c 230 § 2; 1939 c 204 § 3; RRS § 8450-2.]

TITLE 36. COUNTIES
Chapter 36.18 Fees of county officers

RCW 36.18.010 Auditor's fees. County auditors or recording officers shall collect the following fees for their official services:

For recording instruments, for the first page eight and one-half by fourteen inches or less, five dollars; for each additional page eight and one-half by fourteen inches or less, one dollar; the fee for recording multiple transactions contained in one instrument will be calculated individually for each transaction requiring separate indexing as required under RCW 65.04.050;

For preparing and certifying copies, for the first page eight and one-half by fourteen inches or less, three dollars; for each additional page eight and one-half by fourteen inches or less, one dollar;

For preparing noncertified copies, for each page eight and one-half by fourteen inches or less, one dollar;

For administering an oath or taking an affidavit, with or without seal, two dollars;

For issuing a marriage license, eight dollars, (this fee includes taking necessary affidavits, filing returns, indexing, and transmittal of a record of the marriage to the state registrar of vital statistics) plus an additional five-dollar fee for use and support of the prevention of child abuse and neglect activities to be transmitted monthly to the state treasurer and deposited in the state general fund plus an additional ten-dollar fee to be transmitted monthly to the state treasurer and deposited in the state general fund. The legislature intends to appropriate an amount at least equal to the revenue generated by this fee for the purposes of the displaced homemaker act, chapter 28B.04 RCW;

For searching records per hour, eight dollars;

For recording plats, fifty cents for each lot except cemetery plats for which the charge shall be twenty-five cents per lot; also one dollar for each acknowledgment, dedication, and description: PROVIDED, That there shall be a minimum fee of twenty-five dollars per plat;

For recording of miscellaneous records not listed above, for the first page eight and one-half by fourteen inches or less, five dollars; for each additional page eight and one-half by fourteen inches or less, one dollar;

For modernization and improvement of the recording and indexing system, a surcharge as provided in RCW 36.22.170. [1996 c 143 §1; 1995 c 246 §37; 1991 c 26 §2. Prior: 1989 c 304 §1; 1989 c 204 §6; 1987 c 230 §1; 1985 c 44 §2; 1984 c 261 §4; 19821 st ex.s. c 15 §7; 1982 c 4 §12; 1977 ex.s. c 56 §1; 1967 c 26 §8; 1963 c 4 §36. 18.010; prior: 1959 c 263 §6; 1953 c 214 §2; 1951 c 51 §4; 1907 c 56 §1, part, p 92; 1903 c 151 §1, part, p 295; 1893 c 130 §1, part, p 423; Code 1881 §2086, part, p 358; 1869 p 369 §3; 1865 p 94 §1; part; 1863 p 391 §1, part, p 394; 1861 p 34 §1, part, p 37; 1854 p 368 §1, part, p 371; RRS §§497,part, 4105.]

TITLE 42. PUBLIC OFFICERS AND AGENCIES
Chapter 42.20 Misconduct of public officers.

RCW 42.20.020 Powers may not be delegated for profit. Every public officer who, for any reward, consideration or gratuity paid or agreed to be paid, shall, directly or indirectly, grant to another the right or authority to discharge any function of his office, or permit another to perform any of his duties, shall be guilty of a gross misdemeanor. [1909 c 249 §83; RRS §2335.]

Reviser's note: Caption for 1909 c 249 §83 reads as follows: "Sec. 83. Grant of Official Powers."

RCW 42.20.030 Intrusion into and refusal to surrender public office. Every person who shall falsely personate or represent any public officer, or who shall wilfully intrude himself into a public office to which he has not been duly elected or appointed, or who shall wilfully exercise any of the functions or perform any of the duties of such officer, without having duly qualified therefor, as required by law, or who, having been an executive or administrative officer, shall wilfully exercise any of the functions of his office after his right to do so has ceased, or wrongfully refuse to surrender the official seal or any books or papers appertaining to such office, upon the demand of his lawful successor, shall be guilty of a gross misdemeanor. [1909 c 249 §84; RRS §2336.]

NOTES: Impersonating a public officer: RCW 9A.60.040. Quo warranto: Chapter 7.56 RCW.

RCW 42.20.040 False report. Every public officer who shall knowingly make any false or misleading statement in any official report or statement, under circumstances not otherwise prohibited by law, shall be guilty of a gross misdemeanor. [1909 c 249 §98; RRS §2350.]

RCW 42.20.050 Public officer making false certificate. Every public officer who, being authorized by law to make or give a certificate or other writing, shall knowingly make and deliver as true such a certificate or writing containing any statement which he knows to be false, in a case where the punishment thereof is not expressly prescribed by law, shall be guilty of a gross misdemeanor. [1909 c 249 §128; RRS §2380.]

RCW 42.20.100 Failure of duty by public officer a misdemeanor. Whenever any duty is enjoined by law upon any public officer or other person holding any public trust or employment, their wilful neglect to perform such duty, except where otherwise specially provided for, shall be a misdemeanor.

[1909 c 249 §16; RRS §2268. Prior: Code 1881 §889; 1854 p 90 §82.]
NOTES: Official misconduct by public servant: RCW 9A.80.010.

TITLE 62A. UNIFORM COMMERCIAL CODE
Article 3. Negotiable Instruments.
(Formerly: Commercial paper)
Part 5 Dishonor.

RCW 62A.3-501 Presentment. (a) "Presentment" means a demand made by or on behalf of a person entitled to enforce an instrument (i) to pay the instrument made to the drawee or a party obliged to pay the instrument or, in the case of a note or accepted draft payable at a bank, to the bank, or (ii) to accept a draft made to the drawee.

(b) The following rules are subject to Article 4, agreement of the parties, and clearinghouse rules and the like:

(1) Presentment may be made at the place of payment of the instrument and must be made at the place of payment if the instrument is payable at a bank in the United States; may be made by any commercially reasonable means, including an oral, written, or electronic communication; is effective when the demand for payment or acceptance is received by the person to whom presentment is made; and is effective if made to any one of two or more makers, acceptors, drawees, or other payors.

(2) Upon demand of the person to whom presentment is made, the person making presentment must (i) exhibit the instrument, (ii) give reasonable identification and, if presentment is made on behalf of another person, reasonable evidence of authority to do so, and (iii) sign a receipt on the instrument for any payment made or surrender the instrument if full payment is made.

(3) Without dishonoring the instrument, the party to whom presentment is made may (i) return the instrument for lack of a necessary indorsement, or (ii) refuse payment or acceptance for failure of the presentment to comply with the terms of the instrument, an agreement of the parties, or other applicable law or rule.

(4) The party to whom presentment is made may treat presentment as occurring on the next business day after the day of presentment if the party to whom presentment is made has established a cut-off hour not earlier than 2:00 p.m. for the receipt and processing of instruments presented for payment or acceptance and presentment is made after the cut-off hour. [1993c 229 §61; 1965 ex.s. c 157 §3-501. Cf. former RCW sections: RCW 62.01.070, 62.01.089, 62.01.118, 62.01.129, 62.01.143, 62.01.144, 62.01.150, 62.01.151, 62.01.152, 62.01.157, 62.01.158, and 62.01.186; 1955 c 35 §§62.01.070, 62.01.089, 62.01.118, 62.01.129, 62.01.143, 62.01.144, 62.01.150, 62.01.151, 62.01.152, 62.01.157, 62.01.158, and 62.01.186; prior: 1899 c 149 §§70, 89, 118, 129, 143, 144, 150, 151, 152, 157, 158, and 186; RRS §§3461, 3479, 3508, 3519, 3533, 3534, 3540, 3541, 3542, 3547, 3548, and 3576.]

NOTES: Recovery of attorneys' fees—Effective date—1993 c 229: See RCW 62A.11-111 and 62A.11-112.

RCW 62A.3-502 Dishonor. (a) Dishonor of a note is governed by the following rules:

(1) If the note is payable on demand, the note is dishonored if presentment is duly made to the maker and the note is not paid on the day of presentment.

(2) If the note is not payable on demand and is payable at or through a bank or the terms of the note require presentment, the note is dishonored if presentment is duly made and the note is not paid on the day it becomes payable or the day of presentment, whichever is later.

(3) If the note is not payable on demand and subsection (a)(2) does not apply, the note is dishonored if it is not paid on the day it becomes payable.

(b) Dishonor of an unaccepted draft other than a documentary draft is governed by the following rules:

(1) If a check is duly presented for payment to the payor bank otherwise than for immediate payment over the counter, the check is dishonored if the payor bank makes timely return of the check or sends timely notice of dishonor or nonpayment under RCW 62A.4-301or 62A.4-302, or becomes accountable for the amount of the check under RCW 62A.4-302.

(2) If a draft is payable on demand and subsection (b)(1) does not apply, the draft is dishonored if presentment for payment is duly made to the drawee and the draft is not paid on the day of presentment.

(3) If a draft is payable on a date stated in the draft, the draft is dishonored if (i) presentment for payment is duly made to the drawee and payment is not made on the day the draft becomes payable or the day of presentment, whichever is later, or (ii) presentment for acceptance is duly made before the day the draft becomes payable and the draft is not accepted on the day of presentment.

(4) If a draft is payable on elapse of a period of time after sight or acceptance, the draft is dishonored if presentment for acceptance is duly made and the draft is not accepted on the day of presentment.

(c) Dishonor of an unaccepted documentary draft occurs according to the rules stated in subsection (b) (2), (3), and (4), except that payment or acceptance may be delayed without dishonor until no later than the close of the third business day of the drawee following the day on which payment or acceptance is required by subsection (b) (2), (3), and (4).

(d) Dishonor of an accepted draft is governed by the following rules:

(1) If the draft is payable on demand, the draft is dishonored if presentment for payment is duly made to the acceptor and the draft is not paid on the day of presentment; or

(2) If the draft is not payable on demand, the draft is dishonored if presentment for payment is duly made to the acceptor and payment is not made on the day it becomes payable or the day of presentment, whichever is later.

(e) In any case in which presentment is otherwise required for dishonor under this section and presentment is excused under RCW 62A.3-504, dishonor occurs without presentment if the instrument is not duly accepted or paid.

(f) If a draft is dishonored because timely acceptance of the draft was not made and the person entitled to demand acceptance consents to a late acceptance, from the time of acceptance the draft is treated as never having been dishonored. [1993 c 229 §62; 1965 ex.s. c 157 §3-502. Cf. former RCW sections: RCW 62.01.007, 62.01.070, 62.01.089, 62.01.144, 62.01.150, 62.01.152, and 62.01.186; 1955 c 35 §§62.01.007, 62.01.070, 62.01.089,62.01.144, 62.01.150, 62.01.152, and 62.01.186; prior: 1899 c 149 §§7, 70, 89, 144, 150, 152, and 186; RRS §§3398, 3461, 3479, 3534, 3540, 3542, and 3576.]

NOTES: Recovery of attorneys' fees—Effective date—1993 c 229: See RCW 62A.11-111 and 62A.11-112.

RCW 62A.3-503 Notice of dishonor. (a) The obligation of an indorser stated in RCW 62A.3-415(a) and the obligation of a drawer stated in RCW 62A.3-414(d) may not be enforced unless (i) the indorser or drawer is given notice of dishonor of the instrument complying with this section or (ii) notice of dishonor is excused under RCW 62A.3-504(b).

(b) Notice of dishonor may be given by any person; may be given by any commercially reasonable means, including an oral, written, or electronic communication; and is sufficient if it reasonably identifies the instrument and indicates that the instrument has been dishonored or has not been paid or accepted. Return of an instrument given to a bank for collection is sufficient notice of dishonor.

(c) Subject to RCW 62A.3-504(c), with respect to an instrument taken for collection by a collecting bank, notice of dishonor must be given (i) by the bank before midnight of the next banking day following the banking day on which the bank receives notice of dishonor of the instrument, or (ii) by any other person within 30days following the day on which the person receives notice of dishonor. With respect to any other instrument, notice of dishonor must be given within 30 days following the day on which dishonor occurs. [1993 c 229 §63; 1965 ex.s. c 157 §3-503. Cf. former RCW sections: (i) RCW 62.01.071, 62.01.072, 62.01.075, 62.01.086, 62.01.144, 62.01.145, 62.01.146, 62.01.186, and 62.01.193; 1955 c 35 §§62.01.071, 62.01.072, 62.01.075, 62.01.086, 62.01.144, 62.01.145, 62.01.146, 62.01.186, and 62.01.193; prior: 1899 c 149 §§71, 72, 75, 86, 144, 145, 146, 186, and 193; RRS §§3462, 3463, 3466, 3476, 3534, 3535, 3536, 3576, and 3583. (ii) RCW 62.01.085; 1955 c 35 §62.01.085; prior: 1915 c 173 §1; 1899 c 149 §85; RRS §3475 1/2.]

NOTES: Recovery of attorneys' fees—Effective date—1993 c 229: See RCW 62A.11-111 and 62A.11-112.

RCW 62A.3-504 Excused presentment and notice of dishonor. (a) Presentment for payment or acceptance of an instrument is excused if (i) the person entitled to present the instrument cannot with reasonable diligence make presentment, (ii) the maker or acceptor has repudiated an obligation to pay the instrument or is dead or in insolvency proceedings, (iii) by the terms of the instrument presentment is not necessary to enforce the obligation of indorsers or the drawer, (iv) the drawer or indorser whose obligation is being enforced has waived presentment or otherwise has no reason to expect or right to require that the instrument be paid or accepted, or (v) the drawer instructed the drawee not to pay or accept the draft or the drawee was not obligated to the drawer to pay the draft.

(b) Notice of dishonor is excused if (i) by the terms of the instrument notice of dishonor is not necessary to enforce the obligation of a party to pay the instrument, or (ii) the party whose obligation is being enforced waived notice of dishonor. A waiver of presentment is also a waiver of notice of dishonor.

(c) Delay in giving notice of dishonor is excused if the delay was caused by circumstances beyond the control of the person giving the notice and the person giving the notice exercised reasonable diligence after the cause of the delay ceased to operate. [1993 c229 §64; 1965 ex.s. c 157 §3-504. Cf. former RCW sections: RCW 62.01.072, 62.01.073, 62.01.077, 62.01.078, and 62.01.145; 1955 c35 §§62.01.072, 62.01.073, 62.01.077, 62.01.078, and 62.01.145; prior: 1899 c 149 §§72, 73, 77, 78, and 145; RRS §§3463, 3464, 3468, 3469, and 3535.]

NOTES: Recovery of attorneys' fees—Effective date—1993 c 229: See RCW 62A.11-111 and 62A.11-112.

RCW 62A.3-505 Evidence of dishonor. (a) The following are admissible as evidence and create a presumption of dishonor and of any notice of dishonor stated:

(1) A document regular in form as provided in subsection (b) that purports to be a protest;

(2) A purported stamp or writing of the drawee, payor bank, or presenting bank on or accompanying the instrument stating that acceptance or payment has been refused unless reasons for the refusal are stated and the reasons are not consistent with dishonor;

(3) A book or record of the drawee, payor bank, or collecting bank, kept in the usual course of business which shows dishonor, even if there is no evidence of who made the entry.

(b) A protest is a certificate of dishonor made by a United States consul or vice-consul, or a notary public or other person authorized to administer oaths by the law of the place where dishonor occurs. It may be made upon information satisfactory to that person. The protest must identify the instrument and certify either that presentment has been made or, if not made, the reason why it was not made, and that the instrument has been dishonored by nonacceptance or nonpayment. The protest may also certify that notice of dishonor has been given to some or all parties. [1993 c 229 §65; 1965 ex.s. c 157 §3-505. Cf. former RCW sections: (i) RCW 62.01.072(3); 1955 c 35 §62.01.072; prior: 1899 c 149 §72; RRS §3463. (ii) RCW 62.01.074; 1955 c 35 §62.01.074; prior: 1899 c 149 §74; RRS §3465. (iii) RCW 62.01.133; 1955 c 35 §62.01.133; prior: 1899 c 149 §133; RRS §3523.]

NOTES: Recovery of attorneys' fees—Effective date—1993 c 229: See RCW 62A.11-111 and 62A.11-112.

RCW 62A.3-512 Credit cards—As identification—In lieu of deposit. A person may not record the number of a credit card given as identification under *RCW 62A.3-501(a)(2) or given as proof of credit worthiness when payment for goods or services is made by check or draft. Nothing in this section prohibits the recording of the number of a credit card given in lieu of a deposit to secure payment in the event of a default, loss, damage, or other occurrence. [1993 c 229 §66; 1990 c 203 §2.]

*Reviser's note: The reference to RCW 62A.3-501(a)(2) appears erroneous. Reference to RCW 62A.3-501(b)(2) was apparently intended. Recovery of attorneys' fees—Effective date—1993 c 229: See RCW 62A.11-111 and 62A.11-112.

RCW 62A.3-515 Checks dishonored by nonacceptance or nonpayment; liability for interest; rate; collection costs and attorneys' fees; satisfaction of claim. (a) If a check as defined in RCW 62A.3-104 is dishonored by nonacceptance or nonpayment, the payee or holder of the check is entitled to collect a reasonable handling fee for each instrument. If the check is not paid within fifteen days and after the holder of the check sends a notice of dishonor as provided by RCW 62A.3-520 to the drawer at the drawer's last known address, and if the instrument does not provide for the payment of interest or collection costs and attorneys' fees, the drawer of the instrument is liable for payment of interest at the rate of twelve percent per annum from the date of dishonor, and cost of collection not to exceed forty dollars or the face amount of the check, whichever is less. In addition, in the event of court action on the check, the court, after notice and the expiration of the fifteen days, shall award reasonable attorneys' fees, and three times the face amount of the check or three hundred dollars, whichever is less, as part of the damages payable to the holder of the check. This section does not apply to an instrument that is dishonored by reason of a justifiable stop payment order.

(b)(1) Subsequent to the commencement of an action on the check (subsection (a)) but prior to the hearing, the defendant may tender to the plaintiff as satisfaction of the claim, an amount of money equal to the face amount of the check, a reasonable handling fee, accrued interest, collection costs equal to the face amount of the check not to exceed forty dollars, and the incurred court costs, service costs, and statutory attorneys' fees.

(2) Nothing in this section precludes the right to commence action in a court under chapter 12.40 RCW for small claims. [1995 c 187 §1; 1993 c 229 §67; 1991 c 168 §1; 1986 c 128 §1; 1981 c 254 §1; 1969 c 62 §1; 1967 ex.s. c 23 §1.]

NOTES: Recovery of attorneys' fees—Effective date—1993 c 229: See RCW 62A.11-111 and 62A.11-112. Savings—Severability—1967 ex.s. c 23: See notes following RCW 19.52.005.

RCW 62A.3-520 Statutory form for notice of dishonor. The notice of dishonor shall be sent by mail to the drawer at the drawer's last known address, and the notice shall be substantially in the following form:

NOTICE OF DISHONOR OF CHECK
A check drawn by you and made payable by you to _____ in the amount of _____ has not been accepted for payment by _____, which is the drawee bank designated on your check. This check is dated _____, and it is numbered, No._____.

You are CAUTIONED that unless you pay the amount of this check within fifteen days after the date this letter is postmarked, you may very well have to pay the following additional amounts:
(1) Costs of collecting the amount of the check, including an attorney's fee which will be set by the court;
(2) Interest on the amount of the check which shall accrue at the rate of twelve percent per annum from the date of dishonor; and
(3) Three hundred dollars or three times the face amount of the check, whichever is less, by award of the court.
You are also CAUTIONED that law enforcement agencies may be provided with a copy of this notice of dishonor and the check drawn by you for the possibility of proceeding with criminal charges if you do not pay the amount of this check within fifteen days after the date this letter is postmarked.

You are advised to make your payment to _____ at the following address:_____

[1993 c 229 §68; 1991 c 168 §2; 1986 c 128 §2; 1981 c 254 §2; 1969 c 62 §2.]

NOTES: Recovery of attorneys' fees—Effective date—1993 c 229: See RCW 62A.11-111 and 62A.11-112.

RCW 62A.3-522 Notice of dishonor—Affidavit of service by mail. In addition to sending a notice of dishonor to the drawer of the check under RCW 62A.3-520, the holder of the check shall execute an affidavit certifying service of the notice by mail. The affidavit of service by mail must be attached to a copy of the notice of dishonor and must be substantially in the following form:

AFFIDAVIT OF SERVICE BY MAIL
I, _____, hereby certify that on the _____ day of _____, 19___, a copy of the foregoing Notice was served on _____ by mailing via the United States Postal Service, postage prepaid, at _____, Washington.
Dated: _____
_____ (Signature)

The holder shall retain the affidavit with the check but shall file a copy of the affidavit with the clerk of the court in which an action on the check is commenced. [1993 c 229 §69; 1981 c 254 §3.]

NOTES: Recovery of attorneys' fees—Effective date—1993 c 229: See RCW 62A.11-111 and 62A.11-112.

RCW 62A.3-525 Consequences for failing to comply with requirements. No interest, collection costs, and attorneys' fees, except handling fees, are recoverable on any dishonored check under the provisions of RCW 62A.3-515 where the holder of the check or any agent, employee, or assign of the holder has demanded:

(1) Interest or collection costs in excess of that provided by RCW 62A.3-515; or

(2) Interest or collection costs prior to the expiration of fifteen days after the mailing of notice of dishonor, as provided by RCW 62A.3-515 and 62A.3-520; or

(3) Attorneys' fees either without having the fees set by the court, or prior to the expiration of fifteen days after the mailing of notice of dishonor, as provided by RCW 62A.3-515 and 62A.3-520. [1993 c 229 §70; 1981 c 254 §4; 1969 c 62 §3.]

NOTES: Recovery of attorneys' fees—Effective date—1993 c 229: See RCW 62A.11-111 and 62A.11-112.

TITLE 64. REAL PROPERTY AND CONVEYANCES
Chapter 64.08 Acknowledgments.

RCW 64.08.010 Who may take acknowledgments. Acknowledgments of deeds, mortgages and other instruments in writing, required to be acknowledged may be taken in this state before a justice of the supreme court, or the clerk thereof, or the deputy of such clerk, before a judge of the court of appeals, or the clerk thereof, before a judge of the superior court, or qualified court commissioner thereof, or the clerk thereof, or the deputy of such clerk, or a county auditor, or the deputy of such auditor, or a qualified notary public, or a qualified United States commissioner appointed by any district court of the United States for this state, and all said instruments heretofore executed and acknowledged according to the provisions of this section are hereby declared legal and valid. [1971 c 81 §131; 1931 c 13 §1; 1929 c 33 §3; RRS §10559. Prior: 1913 c 14 §1; Code 1881 §2315; 1879 p 110 §1; 1877 p 317 §5; 1875 p 107 §1; 1873 p 466 §5.]

RCW 64.08.020 Acknowledgments out of state—Certificate.

Acknowledgments of deeds conveying or encumbering real estate situated in this state, or any interest therein, and other instruments in writing, required to be acknowledged, may be taken in any other state or territory of the United States, the District of Columbia, or in any possession of the United States, before any person authorized to take the acknowledgments of deeds by the laws of the state, territory, district or possession wherein the acknowledgment is taken, or before any commissioner appointed by the governor of this state, for that purpose, but unless such acknowledgment is taken before a commissioner so appointed by the governor, or before the clerk of a court of record of such state, territory, district or possession, or before a notary public or other officer having a seal of office, the instrument shall have attached thereto a certificate of the clerk of a court of record of the county, parish, or other political subdivision of such state, territory, district or possession wherein the acknowledgment was taken, under the seal of said court, certifying that the person who took the acknowledgment, and whose name is subscribed to the certificate thereof, was at the date thereof such officer as here presented himself to be, authorized by law to take acknowledgments of deeds, and that the clerk verily believes the signature of the person subscribed to the certificate of acknowledgment to be genuine. [1929 c 33 §4; RRS §§10560, 10561. Prior: Code 1881 §§2316, 2317; 1877 p 313 §§6, 7; 1873 p 466 §§6, 7; 1867 pp 93, 94 §§1, 2; 1866 p 89 §1; 1865 p 25 §1. Formerly RCW 64.08.020 and 64.08.030.]

RCW 64.08.040 Foreign acknowledgments, who may take.

Acknowledgments of deeds conveying or encumbering real estate situated in this state, or any interest therein and other instruments in writing, required to be acknowledged, may be taken in any foreign country before any minister, plenipotentiary, secretary of legation, charge d'affaires, consul general, consul, vice consul, consular agent, or commercial agent appointed by the United States government, or before any notary public, or before the judge, clerk, or other proper officer of any court of said country, or before the mayor or other chief magistrate of any city, town or other municipal corporation therein. [1929 c 33 §5; RRS §10563, part. Prior: 1901 c 53 §1; 1888 p 1 §1; Code 1881 §2319; 1875 p 108 §2.]

RCW 64.08.050 Certificate of acknowledgment—Evidence.

The officer, or person, taking an acknowledgment as in this chapter provided, shall certify the same by a certificate written upon or annexed to the instrument acknowledged and signed by him or her and sealed with his or her official seal, if any, and reciting in substance that the person, or persons, known to him or her as, or determined by satisfactory evidence to be, the person, or persons, whose name, or names, are signed to the instrument as executing the same, acknowledged before him or her on the date stated in the certificate that he, she, or they, executed the same freely and voluntarily. Such certificate shall be prima facie evidence of the facts therein recited. The officer or person taking the acknowledgment has satisfactory evidence that a person is the person whose name is signed on the instrument if that person: (1) Is personally known to the officer or person taking the acknowledgment; (2) is identified upon the oath or affirmation of a credible witness personally known to the officer or person taking the acknowledgment; or (3) is identified on the basis of identification documents. [1988 c 69 §1; 1929 c 33 §6; RRS §§10564, 10565. Prior: Code 1881 §§2320, 2321; 1879 p 158 §§2,3.]

RCW 64.08.060 Form of certificate for individual. A certificate of acknowledgment for an individual, substantially in the following form or, after December 31, 1985, substantially in the form set forth in RCW 42.44.100(1), shall be sufficient for the purposes of this chapter and for any acknowledgment required to betaken in accordance with this chapter:

State of _____ ss.
County of _____
On this day personally appeared before me (here insert the name of grantor or grantors) to me known to be the individual, or individuals described in and who executed the within and foregoing instrument, and acknowledged that he (she or they) signed the same as his (her or their) free and voluntary act and deed, for the uses and purposes therein mentioned. Given under my hand and official seal this _____ day of _____, 19____
(Signature of officer and official seal)

If acknowledgment is taken before a notary public of this state the signature shall be followed by substantially the following: Notary Public in and for the state of Washington, residing at _____, (giving place of residence). [1988c 69 §2; 1929 c 33 §13; RRS §10566. Prior: 1888 p 51 §2; 1886 p 179 §7.]

RCW 64.08.070 Form of certificate for corporation. A certificate of acknowledgment for a corporation, substantially in the following form or, after December 31, 1985, substantially in the form set forth in RCW 42.44.100(2), shall be sufficient for the purposes of this chapter and for any acknowledgment required to betaken in accordance with this chapter:

State of _____ ss.
County of _____
On this _____ day of _____, 19____, before me personally appeared _____, to me known to be the (president, vice president, secretary, treasurer, or other authorized officer or agent, as the case may be) of the corporation that executed the within and foregoing instrument, and acknowledged said instrument to be the free and voluntary act and deed of said corporation, for the uses and purposes therein mentioned, and on oath stated that he was authorized to execute said instrument and that the seal affixed is the corporate seal of said corporation.
In Witness Whereof I have hereunto set my hand and affixed my official seal the day and year first above written. (Signature and title of officer with place of residence of notary public.)

[1988 c 69 §3; 1929 c 33 §14; RRS §10567. Prior: 1903 c 132 §1.]

RCW 64.08.090 Authority of superintendents, business managers and officers of correctional institutions to take acknowledgments and administer oaths—Procedure. The superintendents, associate and assistant superintendents, business managers, records officers and camp superintendents of any correctional institution or facility operated by the state of Washington are hereby authorized and empowered to take acknowledgments on any instruments of writing, and certify the same in the manner required by law, and to administer all oaths required by law to be administered, all of the foregoing acts to have the same effect as if performed by a notary public: PROVIDED, That such authority shall only extend to taking acknowledgments for and administering oaths to officers, employees and residents of such institutions and facilities. None of the individuals herein empowered to take acknowledgments and administer oaths shall demand or accept any fee or compensation whatsoever for administering or taking any oath, affirmation, or acknowledgment under the authority conferred by this section.

In certifying any oath or in signing any instrument officially, an individual empowered to do so under this section shall, in addition to his name, state in writing his place of residence, the date of his action, and affix the seal of the institution where he is employed: PROVIDED, That in certifying any oath to be used in any of the courts of this state, it shall not be necessary to append an impression of the official seal of the institution. [1972 ex.s. c 58 §1.]

RCW 64.08.100 Acknowledgments by persons unable to sign name. Any person who is otherwise competent but is physically unable to sign his or her name or make a mark may make an acknowledgment authorized under this chapter by orally directing the notary public or other authorized officer taking the acknowledgment to sign the person's name on his or her behalf. In taking an acknowledgment under this section, the notary public or other authorized officer shall, in addition to stating his or her name and place of residence, state that the signature in the acknowledgment was obtained under the authority of this section. [1987 c 76 §2.]

TITLE 65. RECORDING, REGISTRATION, AND LEGAL PUBLICATION
Chapter 65.04 Duties of county auditor

RCW 65.04.045 Recorded instruments—Requirements—Form. (1) When any instrument is presented to a county auditor or recording officer for recording, the first page of the instrument shall contain:

(a) A top margin of at least three inches and a one-inch margin on the bottom and sides, except that an instrument may be recorded if a minor portion of a notary seal, incidental writing, or minor portion of a signature extends beyond the margins;

(b) The top left-hand side of the page shall contain the name and address to whom the instrument will be returned;

(c) The title or titles, or type or types, of the instrument to be recorded indicating the kind or kinds of documents or transactions contained therein immediately below the three-inch margin at the top of the page. The auditor or recording officer shall be required to index only the title or titles captioned on the document;

(d) Reference numbers of documents assigned or released with reference to the document page number where additional references can be found, if applicable;

(e) The names of the grantor(s) and grantee(s), as defined under RCW 65.04.015, with reference to the document page number where additional names are located, if applicable;

(f) An abbreviated legal description of the property, and for purposes of this subsection, "abbreviated legal description of the property" means lot, block, plat, or section, township, range, and quarter/quarter section, and reference to the document page number where the full legal description is included, if applicable;

(g) The assessor's property tax parcel or account number set forth separately from the legal description or other text.

(2) All pages of the document shall be on sheets of paper of a weight and color capable of producing a legible image that are not larger than fourteen inches long and eight and one-half inches wide with text printed or written in eight point type or larger. All text within the document must be of sufficient color and clarity to ensure that when the text is imaged all text is readable. Further, all pages presented for recording must have at minimum a one-inch margin on the top, bottom, and sides for all pages except page one, except that an instrument may be recorded if a minor portion of a notary seal, incidental writing, or minor portion of a signature extends beyond the margins, be prepared in ink color capable of being imaged, and have all seals legible and capable of being imaged. No attachments, except firmly attached bar code or address labels, may be affixed to the pages....

Washington Administrative Code
Chapter 308-30
NOTARIES PUBLIC

Section	
308-30-005	Mailing address.
308-30-010	Size and form of notary seal or stamp.
308-30-020	Maximum fees that may be charged by notaries public.
308-30-030	Applications for appointment as notary public.
308-30-040	Resignation or revocation of notary appointment.
308-30-050	Replacement of lost or stolen notary seals or stamps.
308-30-060	Department to be notified of change of name or address.
308-30-070	Requests for evidence of authenticity.
308-30-080	Appeals of denials and revocations of notary appointments.
308-30-090	Forms.
308-30-100	Fees.
308-30-120	Notary signature.
308-30-130	Expired stamp or seal.
308-30-140	Notification of legal actions.
308-30-150	Continuous qualification required.
308-30-155	Satisfactory evidence of identity.
308-30-160	Testimonials.
308-30-170	Application of brief adjudicative proceedings.

WASHINGTON NOTARY LAW PRIMER

308-30-180   Preliminary record in brief adjudicative proceedings.
308-30-190   Conduct of brief adjudicative proceedings.

WAC 308-30-005 Mailing address. All correspondence is to be directed to the Department of Licensing, Professional Licensing Services, Notary Section, Post Office Box 9027 (in person 2424 Bristol Court) Olympia, Washington 98507-9027. [Statutory Authority: RCW 42.44.190. 93-05-009, § 308-30-005, filed 2/5/93, effective 3/8/93.]

WAC 308-30-010 Size and form of notary seal or stamp. A notary seal shall be one and five-eighths inches minimum in diameter. If a notary stamp is used the following requirements shall apply:
(1) The type shall be a minimum of 8 point type.
(2) The stamp shall be minimum one and five-eighths inches in diameter. If a rectangular stamp is used the minimum dimensions shall be one inch wide by one and five-eighths inches long.
(3) The imprint shall be affixed with indelible ink only.
(4) The face of any notary stamp shall contain permanently affixed letters and numerals and shall not be preprinted.
(5) The use of the Washington state seal on the notary stamp or seal is prohibited.
(6) A vendor may not provide a notarial seal, or stamp, either inking or embossing, to a person claiming to be a notary, unless the person presents a photo copy of the person's Notary Certificate.
(7) A notary applying for a seal or stamp as a result of a name change shall present a copy to the vendor of the certificate evidencing the notary's name change from the director. [Statutory Authority: RCW 42.44.190. 93-05-009, § 308-30-010, filed 2/5/93, effective 3/8/93. Statutory Authority: 1985 c 156 §§ 5 and 20. 85-24-025 (Order PL 571), § 308-30-010, filed 11/26/85, effective 1/1/86.]

WAC 308-30-020 Maximum fees that may be charged by notaries public. A notary public need not charge fees for notarial services. When fees are charged, notaries shall display in a prominent place, at the place of business, to the public, an English language schedule of fees for notarial acts. No part of the displayed notarial fee schedule may be printed in smaller than 10 pt. type. The following are the maximum fees that may be charged by notaries public for the following services:
(1) Witnessing or attesting a signature with or without seal or stamp, five dollars.
(2) Taking acknowledgment, or verification upon oath or affirmation, five dollars for the first two persons and five dollars for each additional person.
(3) Certifying or attesting a copy, with or without seal or stamp, five dollars.
(4) Receiving or noting a protest of a negotiable instrument, five dollars.
(5) Being present at demand, tender, or deposit, and noting the same, besides mileage at the rate of one dollar per mile, five dollars.
(6) For copying any instrument or record, per page, besides certificate and seal or stamp, one dollar for the first page and twenty-five cents for each remaining page.
(7) Administering an oath or affirmation, five dollars.
(8) Certifying that an event has occurred or an act has been performed, five

WASHINGTON LAWS PERTAINING TO NOTARIES PUBLIC

dollars. [Statutory Authority: RCW 42.44.190. 93-05-009, § 308-30-020, filed 2/5/93, effective 3/8/93. Statutory Authority: 1985 c 156 §§ 5 and 20. 85-24-025 (Order PL 571), § 308-30-020, filed 11/26/85, effective 1/1/86.]

WAC 308-30-030 Applications for appointment as notary public. Applications for appointment as notary public may be obtained from the department of licensing. Every application submitted for appointment as a notary public must be accompanied by the required surety bond and the prescribed fee and shall in all ways comply with the requirements of chapter 42.44 RCW. [Statutory Authority: RCW 42.44.190. 93-05-009, § 308-30-030, filed 2/5/93, effective 3/8/93. Statutory Authority: 1985 c 156 §§ 5 and 20. 85-24-025 (Order PL 571), § 308-30-030, filed 11/26/85, effective 1/1/86.]

WAC 308-30-040 Resignation or revocation of notary appointment. Voluntary resignation by a notary public shall be submitted in writing to the department of licensing. If a notary public voluntarily resigns his or her notary appointment or if the notary appointment is revoked, suspended or restricted, the notary public must mail or deliver his or her notary stamp or seal to the department of licensing. No voluntary resignation of a notary appointment shall be effective until the notary seal or stamp is mailed or delivered to the notary section. [Statutory Authority: RCW 42.44.190. 93-05-009, § 308-30-040, filed 2/5/93, effective 3/8/93. Statutory Authority: 1985 c 156 §§ 5 and 20. 85-24-025 (Order PL 571), § 308-30-040, filed 11/26/85, effective 1/1/86.]

WAC 308-30-050 Replacement of lost or stolen notary seals or stamps. When a notary seal or stamp is lost or stolen the department of licensing is to be notified by certified mail. The notice must set forth the fact that the notary seal or stamp has been lost or stolen and be signed by the notary public. The notary public may then obtain a replacement notary seal or stamp. The new notary seal or stamp must contain some variance from the original seal or stamp. If the lost or stolen notary seal or stamp is found or recovered after a replacement has been obtained the original seal or stamp shall be surrendered to the department of licensing. [Statutory Authority: RCW 42.44.190. 93-05-009, § 308-30-050, filed 2/5/93, effective 3/8/93. Statutory Authority: 1985 c 156 §§ 5 and 20. 85-24-025 (Order PL 571), § 308-30-050, filed 11/26/85, effective 1/1/86.]

WAC 308-30-060 Department to be notified of change of name or address. When a notary public changes his or her name or address, the department of licensing must be notified in writing of such name and/or address change. The notification of name change must be accompanied by a bond rider from the bonding company amending the notary bond, and the prescribed fee for a name change which provides a duplicate notary certificate showing the new name. There is no charge for an address change. [Statutory Authority: RCW 42.44.190. 93-05-009, § 308-30-060, filed 2/5/93, effective 3/8/93. Statutory Authority: 1985 c 156 §§ 5 and 20. 85-24-025 (Order PL 571), § 308-30-060, filed 11/26/85, effective 1/1/86.]

WAC 308-30-070 Requests for evidence of authenticity. Requests for evidences of authenticity of notarial commission must be in writing, accompanied

WASHINGTON NOTARY LAW PRIMER

by the prescribed fee, the original document, and mailed to the department of licensing. [Statutory Authority: RCW 42.44.190. 93-05-009, § 308-30-070, filed 2/5/93, effective 3/8/93. Statutory Authority: 1985 c 156 §§ 5 and 20. 85-24-025 (Order PL 571), § 308-30-070, filed 11/26/85, effective 1/1/86.]

WAC 308-30-080 Appeals of denials and revocations of notary appointments. Notices of appeals of denials and revocations of notary appointments must be in writing and mailed or delivered to the department of licensing. The written notification of appeal must be received by the department within twenty days of the date of denial or revocation or the right to appeal is waived. When the notification of appeal is mailed, the postmarked date will be accepted as the date of receipt by the department of licensing. Procedures on appeal will be as provided in the Administrative Procedure Act, chapter 34.05 RCW, and rules adopted thereunder. [Statutory Authority: RCW 42.44.190. 93-05-009, § 308-30-080, filed 2/5/93, effective 3/8/93. Statutory Authority: 1985 c 156 §§ 5 and 20. 85-24-025 (Order PL 571), § 308-30-080, filed 11/26/85, effective 1/1/86.]

WAC 308-30-090 Forms. (1) The forms in RCW 42.44.100 are only suggested certificates with the sufficient information included. These forms may be used; however, when a specific form is required by a specific statute, the required form shall be used.

(2) A nonattorney notary may complete notarial certificates, and may not assist another person in drafting, completing, selecting, or understanding a document or transaction requiring a notarial act. This does not preclude a notary who is duly qualified in a particular profession from giving advice relating to matters in that professional field. [Statutory Authority: RCW 42.44.190. 93-05-009, § 308-30-090, filed 2/5/93, effective 3/8/93. Statutory Authority: 1985 c 156 §§ 5 and 20. 85-24-025 (Order PL 571), § 308-30-090, filed 11/26/85, effective 1/1/86.]

WAC 308-30-100 Fees. The following fees shall be charged by the director of the department of licensing: Title of Fee Fee Application for notary appointment $20.00 Renewal of notary appointment 20.00 Duplicate certificate of appointment 15.00 (including change of name) Evidence of verification of notarial 15.00 commission* Apostille 15.00 [Statutory Authority: RCW 43.24.086. 90-06-052, § 308-30-100, filed 3/2/90, effective 4/2/90. Statutory Authority: 1985 c 156 §§ 5 and 20. 85-24-025 (Order PL 571), § 308-30-100, filed 11/26/85, effective 1/1/86.]

WAC 308-30-120 Notary signature. Upon completion of a notarial act, the notary must sign the notary certification using his/her name exactly as it appears on the notary certificate of appointment and the stamp or seal. The notary's name must be legibly printed or stamped directly below their signature. [Statutory Authority: RCW 42.44.190. 93-05-009, § 308-30-120, filed 2/5/93, effective 3/8/93.]

WAC 308-30-130 Expired stamp or seal. The use of a stamp or seal with an expired date is prohibited. [Statutory Authority: RCW 42.44.190. 93-05-009, § 308-30-130, filed 2/5/93, effective 3/8/93.]

---

* As in original. This sentence probably should read "Evidence of verification of notarial commission, 15.00".

WASHINGTON LAWS PERTAINING TO NOTARIES PUBLIC

WAC 308-30-140 Notification of legal actions. The notary must notify the department of licensing of any conviction against him or her of official misconduct, and/or civil or criminal charges. Notification must be submitted within thirty days of such happening. [Statutory Authority: RCW 42.44.190. 93-05-009, § 308-30-140, filed 2/5/93, effective 3/8/93.]

WAC 308-30-150 Continuous qualification required. A notary public must continue to meet the requirements of RCW 42.44.020 (1)(b) or (c) throughout the term of appointment. A notary who fails to meet any one or more of the aforementioned requirements shall resign, or the director shall institute hearings to determine if the requirements have been met by the notary. [Statutory Authority: RCW 42.44.190. 93-05-009, § 308-30-150, filed 2/5/93, effective 3/8/93.]

WAC 308-30-155 Satisfactory evidence of identity. Satisfactory evidence of an individual identity shall be based on one of the following:

(1) Current documents issued by a federal or state government with the individual's photograph, signature, and physical description.

(2) The oath or affirmation of a credible person who personally knows the individual. [Statutory Authority: RCW 42.44.190. 93-05-009, § 308-30-155, filed 2/5/93, effective 3/8/93.]

WAC 308-30-160 Testimonials. A notary may not endorse or promote any service, contest, or other offering if the notary's seal or title is used in the endorsement or promotional statement. [Statutory Authority: RCW 42.44.190. 93-05-009, § 308-30-160, filed 2/5/93, effective 3/8/93.]

WAC 308-30-170 Application of brief adjudicative proceedings. The director adopts RCW 34.05.482 through 34.05.494 for the administration of brief adjudicative proceedings conducted by request, and/or at the discretion of the director pursuant to RCW 34.05.482, for the categories of matters set forth below. Brief adjudicative proceedings will be limited to a determination of one or more of the following issues:

(1) Whether an applicant for an appointment meets the minimum criteria for an appointment as a notary public in this state and the department proposes to deny the application;

(2) Whether a person is in compliance with the terms and conditions of a final order or agreement previously issued by the department; and

(3) Whether an appointment holder requesting renewal has submitted all required information and whether an appointment holder meets minimum criteria for renewal. [Statutory Authority: RCW 34.05.410 (1)(a) and 34.05.482 (1)(c). 97-10-052, § 308-30-170, filed 5/1/97, effective 6/1/97.]

WAC 308-30-180 Preliminary record in brief adjudicative proceedings.
(1) The preliminary record with respect to an application for appointment or reappointment shall consist of:

(a) The application for appointment or reappointment and all associated documents;

(b) All documents relied upon by the director in proposing to deny the appointment or reappointment; and

(c) All correspondence between the applicant for appointment or reappointment and the director regarding the application.

(2) The preliminary record with respect to determination of compliance with a previously issued final order or agreement shall consist of:

(a) The previously issued final order or agreement;

(b) All reports or other documents submitted by, or at the direction of, the appointment holder, in full or partial fulfillment of the terms of the final order or agreement;

(c) All correspondence between the appointment holder and the director regarding compliance with the final order or agreement; and

(d) All documents relied upon by the director showing that the appointment holder has failed to comply with the previously issued final order or agreement. [Statutory Authority: RCW 34.05.410 (1)(a) and 34.05.482 (1)(c). 97-10-052, § 308-30-180, filed 5/1/97, effective 6/1/97.]

WAC 308-30-190 Conduct of brief adjudicative proceedings. (1) Brief adjudicative proceedings shall be conducted by a presiding officer for brief adjudicative proceedings designated by the director. The presiding officer for brief adjudicative proceedings shall not have personally participated in the decision which resulted in the request for a brief adjudicative proceeding.

(2) The parties or their representatives may present written documentation. The presiding officer for brief adjudicative proceedings shall designate the date by which written documents must be submitted by the parties.

(3) The presiding officer for brief adjudicative proceedings may, in his or her discretion, entertain oral argument from the parties or their representatives.

(4) No witnesses may appear to testify.

(5) In addition to the record, the presiding officer for brief adjudicative proceedings may employ department expertise as a basis for the decision.

(6) The presiding officer for brief adjudicative proceedings shall not issue an oral order. Within ten days of the final date for submission of materials or oral argument, if any, the presiding officer for brief adjudicative proceedings shall enter an initial order. [Statutory Authority: RCW 34.05.410 (1)(a) and 34.05.482 (1)(c). 97-10-052, § 308-30-190, filed 5/1/97, effective 6/1/97.] ■

Office of the Washington Dept. of Licensing

Department of Licensing
Business & Occupations Unit
Notaries Public Licensing Program

Walk-in Address:
405 Black Lake Blvd., Bldg. 2
Olympia, WA 98507

Mailing Address:
P.O. Box 9027
Olympia, WA 98507-9027

Telephone: 1-360-753-3836
Fax: 1-360-664-2550
E-mail: BNOUNIT@dol.wa.gov

In addition, there are many useful resources available at the state's official Web site, including links to legislative information, the Secretary of State's office and research bureaus. You can access the state's home page at www.state.wa.us.
Information for Notaries appears at the Department of Licensing's Notary page at www.wa.gov/dol/bpd/notfront.htm.

Bureaus of Vital Statistics

Washington Notaries are strongly discouraged from making certified copies of any document that is recordable or a public record. Persons requesting "notarization," "certification" or certified copies of birth or death certificates should be referred to the appropriate public office. The following state agencies can provide certified copies of birth and death records of persons who were born or have died in the respective states, as can certain local offices not listed here:

Alabama
Center for Health Statistics
State Department of Public Health
P.O. Box 5625
Montgomery, AL 36103-5625

Alaska
Department of Health & Social Services
Bureau of Vital Statistics
P.O. Box H-02G
Juneau, AK 99811-0675

Arizona
Vital Records Section
Arizona Dept. of Health Services
P.O. Box 3887
Phoenix, AZ 85030

Arkansas
Division of Vital Records
Arkansas Department of Health
4815 West Markham Street
Little Rock, AR 72201

California
Vital Statistics Section
Department of Health Services
P.O. Box 730241
Sacramento, CA 94244-0241

Colorado
Vital Records Section
Colorado Department of Health
4300 Cherry Creek Drive South
Denver, CO 80222-1530

Connecticut
Vital Records
Department of Health Services
150 Washington Street
Hartford, CT 06106

Delaware
Office of Vital Statistics
Division of Public Health
P.O. Box 637
Dover, DE 19903

BUREAUS OF VITAL STATISTICS

District of Columbia
Vital Records Branch
425 I Street, N.W., Room 3009
Washington, DC 20001

Florida
Department of Health &
Rehabilitative Services
Office of Vital Statistics
1217 Pearl Street
P.O. Box 210
Jacksonville, FL 32231

Georgia
Georgia Dept. of Human Resources
Vital Records Unit
Room 217-H
47 Trinity Avenue, S.W.
Atlanta, GA 30334

Hawaii
Office of Health Status Monitoring
State Department of Health
P.O. Box 3378
Honolulu, HI 96801

Idaho
Vital Statistics Unit
Idaho Department of Health
& Welfare
450 West State Street
Statehouse Mail
Boise, ID 83720-9990

Illinois
Division of Vital Records
Illinois Department of Public Health
605 West Jefferson Street
Springfield, IL 62702-5097

Indiana
Vital Records Section
State Department of Health
1330 West Michigan Street
P.O. Box 1964
Indianapolis, IN 46206-1964

Iowa
Iowa Department of
Public Health
Vital Records Section
Lucas Office Building
321 East 12th Street
Des Moines, IA 50319-0075

Kansas
Office of Vital Statistics
Kansas State Department of
Health & Environment
900 Jackson Street
Topeka, KS 66612-1290

Kentucky
Office of Vital Statistics
Department for Health Services
275 East Main Street
Frankfort, KY 40621

Louisiana
Vital Records Registry
Office of Public Health
325 Loyola Avenue
New Orleans, LA 70112

Maine
Office of Vital Statistics
Maine Department of
Human Services
State House Station 11
Augusta, ME 04333-0011

Maryland
Division of Vital Records
Department of Health
and Mental Hygiene
Metro Executive Building
4201 Patterson Ave.
P.O. Box 68760
Baltimore, MD 21215-0020

Massachusetts
Registry of Vital Records
and Statistics
150 Tremont Street, Room B-3
Boston, MA 02111

Michigan
Office of the State Registrar and
Center for Health Statistics
Michigan Department of
Public Health
3423 North Logan Street
Lansing, MI 48909

Minnesota
Minnesota Department of Health
Section of Vital Statistics
717 Delaware Street, S.E.
P.O. Box 9441
Minneapolis, MN 55440

Mississippi
Vital Records
State Department of Health
2423 North State Street.
Jackson, MS 39216

Missouri
Missouri Department of Health
Bureau of Vital Records
1730 East Elm
P.O. Box 570
Jefferson City, MO 65102-0570

Montana
Bureau of Records & Statistics
State Department of Health
& Environmental Services
Helena, MT 59620

Nebraska
Bureau of Vital Statistics
State Department of Health
301 Centennial Mall South
P.O. Box 95007
Lincoln, NE 68509-5007

Nevada
Division of Health — Vital Statistics
Capitol Complex
505 East King Street, #102
Carson City, NV 89710

New Hampshire
Bureau of Vital Records
Health and Welfare Building
6 Hazen Drive
Concord, NH 03301

New Jersey
State Department of Health
Bureau of Vital Statistics
South Warren and Market
CN 370
Trenton, NJ 08625

New Mexico
Vital Statistics
New Mexico Health Services
Division
P.O. Box 26110
Santa Fe, NM 87502

New York State
Vital Records Section
State Department of Health
Empire State Plaza
Tower Building
Albany, NY 12237-0023

New York City
Division of Vital Records
New York City Department
of Health
P.O. Box 3776
New York, NY 10007

North Carolina
Department of Environment,
Health and Natural Resources
Division of Epidemiology
Vital Records Section
225 North McDowell Street
P.O. Box 29537
Raleigh, NC 27626-0537

North Dakota
Division of Vital Records
State Capitol
600 East Boulevard Avenue
Bismarck, ND 58505

Ohio
Bureau of Vital Statistics
Ohio Department of Health
P.O. Box 15098
Columbus, OH 43215-0098

BUREAUS OF VITAL STATISTICS

Oklahoma
Vital Records Section
State Department of Health
1000 Northeast 10th Street,
P.O. Box 53551
Oklahoma City, OK 73152

Oregon
Oregon Health Division
Vital Statistics Section
P.O. Box 14050
Portland, OR 97214-0050

Pennsylvania
Division of Vital Records
State Department of Health
Central Building
101 S. Mercer Street, P.O. Box 1528
New Castle, PA 16103

Rhode Island
Division of Vital Records
Rhode Island Department of Health
Room 101, Cannon Building
3 Capitol Hill
Providence, RI 02908-5097

South Carolina
Office of Vital Records & Public Health Statistics
South Carolina Department of Health & Environmental Control
2600 Bull Street
Columbia, SC 29201

South Dakota
State Department of Health
Center for Health Policy and Statistics
Vital Records
523 East Capitol
Pierre, SD 57501

Tennessee
Tennessee Vital Records
Department of Health
Cordell Hull Building
Nashville, TN 37247-0350

Texas
Bureau of Vital Statistics
Texas Department of Health
1100 West 49th Street
Austin, TX 78756-3191

Utah
Bureau of Vital Records
Utah Department of Health
288 North 1460 West
P.O. Box 16700
Salt Lake City, UT 84116-0700

Vermont
Vermont Department of Health
Vital Records Section
60 Main Street, Box 70
Burlington, VT 05402

Virginia
Division of Vital Records
State Health Department
P.O. Box 1000
Richmond, VA 23208-1000

Washington
Department of Health
Center for Health Statistics
P.O. Box 9709
Olympia, WA 98507-9709

West Virginia
Vital Registration Office
Division of Health
State Capitol Complex
Building 3
Charleston, WV 25305

Wisconsin
Vital Records
1 West Wilson Street
P.O. Box 309
Madison, WI 53701

Wyoming
Vital Records Services
Hathaway Building
Cheyenne, WY 82002

American Samoa
Registrar of Vital Statistics
Vital Statistics Section
Government of American Samoa
Pago Pago, AS 96799

Guam
Office of Vital Statistics
Department of Public Health
& Social Services
Government of Guam
P.O. Box 2816
Agana, GU, M.I. 96910

Northern Mariana Islands
Superior Court
Vital Records Section
P.O. Box 307
Saipan, MP 96950

Panama Canal Zone
Panama Canal Commission
Vital Statistics Clerk
APOAA 34011

Puerto Rico
Department of Health
Demographic Registry
P.O. Box 11854
Fernández Juncos Station
San Juan, PR 00910

Virgin Islands (St. Croix)
Registrar of Vital Statistics
Charles Harwood Memorial Hospital
Christiansted, St. Croix, VI 00820

Virgin Islands (St. Thomas, St. John)
Registrar of Vital Statistics
Knud Hansen Complex
Hospital Ground
Charlotte Amalie
St. Thomas, VI 00802

Hague Convention Nations

The nations listed on the following pages are parties to a treaty called the Hague Convention Abolishing the Requirement of Legalization (Authentication) for Foreign Public Documents.

Treaty Simplifies Authentication. A Notary's signature on documents that are sent to these nations may be authenticated by the Washington Department of Licensing through attachment of a single certificate of capacity called an *apostille*. The *apostille* (French for "notation") is the only authentication certificate necessary. Nations not subscribing to the Hague Convention may require as many as five or six separate authenticating certificates from different governmental agencies, domestic and foreign.

How to Request an *Apostille*. To obtain an *apostille*, mail or present in person a written request, the original notarized document, the Notary's name and commission expiration date, and a $15 fee per document in a check payable to the "Washington State Treasurer" to:

Department of Licensing, Business & Occupations Unit
Notary Public Licensing Program
P.O. Box 9027
Olympia, WA 98507-9027
1-360-753-3836

An *apostille* must be specifically requested, indicating the nation to which the document will be sent.
It is *not* the Notary's responsibility to obtain an *apostille*, but rather, it is the responsibility of the party sending the document.

Hague Convention Nations. The following nations participate in the Hague Convention:

Andorra	El Salvador
Angola[1]	Fiji
Antigua and Barbuda	Finland
Argentina[2]	France[5]
Armenia[3]	Germany
Australia	Greece
Austria	Grenada[1]
Bahamas	Guyana
Barbados	Hong Kong[6]
Belarus[3]	Hungary
Belgium	Israel
Belize	Italy
Bosnia-Herzegovina[4]	Japan
Botswana	Kiribati[1]
Brunei	Latvia
Comoros Islands[1]	Lesotho
Croatia[4]	Liberia[7]
Cyprus	Liechtenstein
Djibouti[1]	Luxembourg
Dominica[1]	Macedonia[4]

1. Recently independent country; has not confirmed that the Convention still applies. In accordance with Article 34(l) of the Vienna Convention on Succession of States in Respect of Treaties, the United States' view is that when a country is a party to a multilateral treaty or convention, and that country dissolves, the successor states inherit the treaty obligations of the former government.

2. Excludes recognition of extension of the Convention by the United Kingdom to the Malvinas, South Georgia, South Sandwich Islands and the Argentine Antarctic Sector.

3. Now known as the Newly Independent States. Former Union of Soviet Socialist Republics (U.S.S.R.) had signed on to the Convention, but dissolved prior to its taking effect. Only Armenia, the Belarus Republic and the Russian Federation of the former U.S.S.R. have confirmed that the Convention applies in their jurisdictions.

4. Former Yugoslavia, with its capital in the present Serbia-Montenegro, was a party to the Convention. However, only the breakaway nations of Bosnia-Herzegovina, Croatia, Macedonia and Slovenia have confirmed that the Convention still applies.

5. Including French Overseas Departments of French Guiana, French Polynesia, Guadeloupe, Martinique, New Caledonia, Reunion, St. Pierre and Miquelon, and Wallis and Futuna.

6. Retained status as Hague nation after control of Hong Kong was returned to China on July 1, 1997.

7. Convention does *not* apply between Liberia and the United States.

HAGUE CONVENTION NATIONS

Malawi	San Marino, Republic of
Malta	Seychelles
Marshall Islands	Slovenia[4]
Mauritius	Solomon Islands[1]
Mexico	South Africa
Mozambique[1]	Spain
Netherlands[8]	Suriname
Norway	Swaziland
Panama	Switzerland
Portugal[9]	Turkey
Russia[3]	Tuvalu[1]
Saint Kitts and Nevis	United Kingdom[10]
Saint Lucia	United States
Saint Vincent and the Grenadines	of America
	Vanuatu[1]

Inquiries. Persons having questions about the Hague Convention Abolishing the Requirement of Legalization for Foreign Public Documents may address their inquiries to:

> Office of American Citizen Services
> Department of State
> Washington, D.C. 20520
> 1-202-647-5225

---

1. Recently independent country; has not confirmed that the Convention still applies. In accordance with Article 34(l) of the Vienna Convention on Succession of States in Respect of Treaties, the United States' view is that when a country is a party to a multilateral treaty or convention, and that country dissolves, the successor states inherit the treaty obligations of the former government.

3. Now known as the Newly Independent States. Former Union of Soviet Socialist Republics (U.S.S.R.) had signed on to the Convention, but dissolved prior to its taking effect. Only Armenia, the Belarus Republic and the Russian Federation of the former U.S.S.R. have confirmed that the Convention applies in their jurisdictions.

4. Former Yugoslavia, with its capital in the present Serbia-Montenegro, was a party to the Convention. However, only the breakaway nations of Bosnia-Herzegovina, Croatia, Macedonia and Slovenia have confirmed that the Convention still applies.

8. Extended to Aruba, Curacao and Netherlands Antilles.

9. Extended to Macao and all overseas territories.

10. United Kingdom of Great Britain and Northern Ireland is extended to Anguilla, Bermuda, British Antarctica Territory, British Virgin Islands, Cayman Islands, Falkland Islands, Gibraltar, Guernsey, Isle of Man, Jersey, Montserrat, Saint Georgia and the South Sandwich Islands, Saint Helena, Tonga, Turks and Caicos Islands, and Zimbabwe.

About the Publisher

Founded in 1957, the National Notary Association is a professional, nonprofit organization dedicated to imparting knowledge, understanding and unity among Notaries and instilling in them only the highest standards of ethical conduct and sound notarial practice.

As the nation's clearinghouse for information on notarial laws, customs and practices, the NNA educates Notaries about the legal, ethical and technical facets of performing a notarial act, through its publications, seminars and an annual conference.

As the preeminent publisher of instructional literature on notarization, the Association authors and issues a wide range of educational resources. It also provides Notaries with the highest quality professional support systems, through the design, development and manufacturing of products such as official seals and stamps, recordkeeping journals, thumbprinting devices and certificates.

Promoting procedures that deter impropriety, injustice and fraud, the NNA supports uniform, modern and effective laws in all states through promulgation of its *Model Notary Act*, and serves as a notarial information center for officials, legislators, educators and the public at large.

As it strives to preserve and cultivate appreciation for the rich heritage and tradition of the Notary office, the NNA works to instill among Notaries a sense of self-respect and professional pride, while increasing the public's awareness and understanding of their vital function in modern society. ■

Index

A

Acknowledgment 22, **23–28**, 77–78, *79–80, 97*
   Acknowledge signature. 24
   Capacity of signer 24–25
   Certificates for **25–26**, *79–80, 97*
   Common act 23
   Date 15
   Defined 75
   Fees **51**, *100*
   Identification of signer . . 25, 27, 38, 77–78
   Purpose **23–24**, 77–78
   Requirements **24**, 77–78
   Terminology 27
   Who may take. **27–28**, *95–96, 98*
   Witnessing signature . 11–12, **27**
Act, certifying event or 23, **35–36**, 77–78, *80*
   Certificate **36**, *80*
   Purpose. **35**, 77–78
Address, change of . .**21**, *101, 103*
Advertising,
   foreign-language 58–59

Advice (see Law, unauthorized practice of) 16–17, **54–55**, 83–84, *102*
Affidavit 30–31
Affirmation 23, **32–34**, 75
   Ceremony. 33–34
   Corporate affirmations . . . 32–33
   Credible identifying witnesses, for 33, **40**
   Defined. 32
   Deposition, for. 30
   Fees **52**, *100–101*
   Gestures. 33–34
   Jurat, for 31
   Power to administer. . . . **32**, 75
   Purpose 32
   Response required 33
   Verification, for **31**, 75
   Wording 33
Apostilles **57–58**, *82,* 111–113
Appearance, personal . . . **13**, 65, *82, 89*
Attesting signature . . .22, **31–32**, 77–78, *79–80*
   Certificate **32**, *79–80*
   Purpose. **31–32**, *79–80*

Page numbers listed in **bold** indicate where the most complete information on a subject can be found. *Italics* indicate the pages where the statutes pertaining to a subject are located.

Authentication **57–58**, 82, *101–102*
Apostilles **57–58**, 82, 111–113
Fees **57–58**, *102*
Hague Convention Abolishing the Requirement of Legalization for Foreign Public Documents 57–58, **111–113**
Hague Convention nations........... 112–113
Out of state 57–58
Out of country........... 58
Procedure........... 57–58
Authority, certificate of (see Authentication) **57–58**, 82, *101–102*

B

Beneficial interest (see Disqualifying interest) ...9, 11, 34, 40, 51, **53**, 61–62
Birth certificate, certified copy of **11**, 29, 106
Blank spaces in document .14, **54**
Bond, Notary 4, **19–20**, 76
Liability of Notary 20
Liability of surety 20
Purpose 20
Bureaus of Vital Statistics 106–110

C

Capacity, certificate of (see Authentication) **57–58**, 82, *101–102*
Capacity of signer 15, **24–25**, 39, 42
Certificates, notarial 7, 15–16, 25–26, 29, 31, 32, 35, 36, 37–38, **43–48**, 79–80, 97

Acknowledgment, for... **25–26**, 46–47, 79–80, 97
Act, certifying ... **36**, 48, 79–80
Affidavit, for.... **31**, 47, 79–80
Attesting signature, for .. **32**, 47, 79–80
Attorney in fact, for **26**, 79
Certified copy, for **29**, 48, 79–80
Certifying event or act 36
Choosing........... 15–16, 16–17, **46**, *102*
Contents............. 43–44
Correcting 10
Deposition, for........ 30, **31**
Event, certifying **36**, 48, 79–80
False........... **48**, *82*, 89
Format requirements.. **45**, *98–99*
Illegibility of **48**, *80*
Jurat......... **31**, 47, 79–80
Loose certificates.... 16, **44–45**
Military personnel, by...... 61
Pre-sign or seal 46
Proof of acknowledgment by subscribing witness.... 35
Protest 37–38
Requirement........... 43–44
Seal of Notary 44
Selecting 15–16, 16–17, **46**, *102*
Short-form certificates 26, **46–49**, 79–80
Signature of Notary 44
Size requirements ... **45**, *98–99*
Statement of particulars..... 44
Telegraphic copies..... **48**, *86*
Testimonium clause 44
Venue................. 43
Verification, for .. **31**, 47, 79–80
Witnessing signature, for.......... **32**, 47, 79–80
Certificate of authority (see Authentication) **57–58**, 82, *101–102*

INDEX

Certificate of capacity
(see Authentication) **57–58**, 82, *101–102*
Certificate of official character
(see Authentication) **57–58**, 82, *101–102*
Certificate of prothonotary
(see Authentication) **57–58**, 82, *101–102*
Certified copies 11, 22, **28–29**, *77–78, 80*
  Birth certificate, of 11, **29**
  Certificate for. **29**, *80*
  Death certificate, of 11, **29**
  Fees **51**, *100*
  Precautions 29
  Procedure **28–29**, *78*
  Purpose 28
  Recordable documents, of. . . 28
  Vital records, of 11, **29**
Certifying event or act 23, **35–36**, *78–79, 80*
  Certificate **36**, *80*
  Purpose **35**, *77–78*
Commission, Notary *17–22*
  Address, change of. . . . **21**, *101*
  Application 3–4, **18–19**, *75–76*
  Appointment. . . . **18–19**, *75–76*
  Bond 4, **19–20**, *75–76*
  Denial of. **19**, *76–77*
  Endorsements. . . **19**, *75–76*, 77
  Fees **19**, *102*
  Jurisdiction **20**, 77
  Name, change of . . **21–22**, *101*
  Oath for. 4, **20**, *75–76*
  Personal declaration . **20**, *75–76*
  Qualifications 3, **18–19**, *75–76*

Rejection of application 19, *76–77*
Renewal 4
Resignation **21**, *82, 103*
Revocation. **63**, *82, 103*
Seal 4–5, 16, **49–51**, 77, *78–79, 100–101*
Term. **20–21**, 77
Conformed copy 10
Copy certification (see
Certified copies) 11, 22, **28–29**, *77–78, 80*
Credible identifying
witness 9, 38, **39–40**, *78*
  Affirmation for 33, **40**
  Identification of **39–40**, *78*
  Journal entry 40
  Oath for 33, **40**
  Purpose 39
  Qualifications . . **39–40**, *78, 103*
  Signature in journal 40
  Subscribing witness
confusion 40
Customers, restricting
services to 10

D

Date of document 15
Death certificate, certified
copy of 11, 29
Deposition 22, **29–30**, *85*
  Affirmation for **30**, 33, *85*
  Definition **29–30**, *85*
  Oath for **30**, 33, *85*
  Purpose 29–30
Disabled signer, signing
for **55–56**, *77–78*, 98

Page numbers listed in **bold** indicate where the most complete information on a subject can be found. *Italics* indicate the pages where the statutes pertaining to a subject are located.

117

Certificate **56**, 77–78, *98*
Journal entry 56
Notarization. 56
Disqualifying interest 9, 11,
34, 40,
52–53, *78*
  Beneficial interest 9, 11,
34, 40,
53, 61–62
  Employees. 53
  Financial interest 53
  Relatives 12, **53**
Documents:
  Blank spaces **14**, 54
  Date, checking. 15
  Foreign language. . . . 10–11, **59**
  Incomplete **14**, 54
  Preparation of 16–17,
54–55
  Scan for information 14–15
  Selection of 16–17
Duties **22–23**, *75*

E

Embosser, Notary seal 6,
49–51,
66, 77, *100*
Equipment 6–7
Errors and omissions
  insurance 7
Exam, trial 68–73
Employer **54**, *79*
Event, certifying
  act or 23, **35–36**,
77–78, *80*
  Certificate **36**, *80*
  Purpose. **35**, 77–78

F

Family members, notarizing
  for (see Disqualifying
  interest) 12, **53**
Fees **51–52**, *80*,
87, *100–101*

Acknowledgments, for. **51**,
100–101
Affirmations, for . . **52**, *100–101*
Certified copy, for. . **51**, *100–101*
Certifying event or
  act **51**, *100–101*
Journal entry 42
Maximum **51–52**, *100–101*
Oaths, for. **52**, *100–101*
Option not to charge . . . **52**, *80*
Overcharging **52**, *87*,
100–101
Posting **52**, *100–101*
Proof of
  acknowledgment 52
Protests, for **52**, *100–101*
Record of 42
Signature, witness or
  attest. **52**, *100–101*
Travel **52**, *100–101*
Verification, for. . . **51**, *100–101*
Financial interest (see
  Disqualifying interest) . . .11, 34,
40, **53**
Foreign languages . . 10–11, **58–60**
  Advertising 58–59
  Documents 10–11, **59**
  Signers 10–11, **59–60**
  Translating Notary Public . . . 59
Flags (see
  Authentication) **57–58**,
82, *101–102*

H

Hague Convention Abolishing the
Requirement of Legalization
for Foreign Public
Documents . . .57–58, **111–113**

I

Identification 13, **38–41**,
75, 77–78, *103*
Acknowledgment, for. . . 27, **38**,
77–78, *103*

INDEX

Capacity of signer. . . 25, **39**, *75*
Credible identifying
   witness. 9, **39–40**,
                         77–78, 103
   Documents **40–41**,
                         77–78, 103
   Journal entry 42
   Jurat, for 31, **38**
   Minors, of 57
   Other notarial acts, for 38
   Personal knowledge **39**,
                               77–78
   Representative signer . . . **25**, *75*
   Satisfactory evidence **36**,
                              88, 103
   Verification, for. 31, **38**
Identification documents . . **40–41**,
                         77–78, 103
   Acceptable **40–41**,
                         77–78, 103
   Fraudulent. 41
   Multiple 41
   Immigration 60
   Advice 60
   Documents 60
   Naturalization
     certificates. 60
Impartiality (see Disqualifying
   interest) 9, 11, 34,
                      40, **52–53**, *78*
Incomplete documents . . .14, **54**
Insurance, errors and
   omissions 7

J

Journal of notarial acts 6–7,
                         15, **41–43**
   Credible identifying witness,
     entry for 42
   Entries, additional 42–43
   Entries required. . . . 6–7, 15, **42**

Recommendation 41–42
Signature by mark,
   entry for 55
Thumbprint. 7
Jurat (see Verification) 22,
                       30–31, *75,*
                   77–78, 79–80
Jurisdiction **20**, 77

K

Knowledge, of
   identity, personal . . .**39**, *77–78*

L

Law, unauthorized
   practice of **54–55**, 60,
                          61–62, 64,
                          83–84, 102
   Advice. 16–17,
                      54–55, 61, 64
   Assistance. 54–55
   Blanks in document 14, **54**
   Exceptions **55**, *102*
   Preparing document 16–17,
                             54–55
   Selecting notarization . . . 15–16,
                              16–17,
                           46, *102*
Laws pertaining to
   notarization *74–104*
Legalization
   (see Authentication) **57–58**,
                        82, 101–102
Liability 16–17, **20**, 67
   Notary, of 20
   Surety, of 20
Living wills 62
Locus sigilli **44**, 50
Loose certificates 16, **44–45**
L.S. **44**, 50

Page numbers listed in **bold** indicate where the most complete information on a subject can be found. *Italics* indicate the pages where the statutes pertaining to a subject are located.

119

M

Mark, signature by 55
   Procedures 55
   Witnesses 55
   Witness jurat 55
Marriages 23, **56–57**
Military-personnel,
   notarizations by 60–61
Minors, notarizing for 57
   Identification 57
   Signature................ 57
Misconduct **62–67**, 75,
               76–77, 82,
             83–84, 86–87,
              89–90, 103
   Advice............... 16–17,
           54–55, 61, 64
   Assistance............. 54–55
   Certificate, false....... **64–65**,
                  82, 89
   Defined **62**, 76–77, 82
   Denial of appointment.. 19, **63**,
                67, 76–77
   Document, completing
      false.............. **65**, 86
   Duty, allowing another
      to perform **66**, 89
   Duty, failure to perform.... **66**,
                  87–88
   Endorsement **65**, 103
   Fees, failure to post **65**,
                 100–101
   Felony conviction... **64**, 76–77
   Impersonating a
      Notary **64**, 82
   Incompetence of
      Notary **63**, 82
   Law, unauthorized
      practice of....... 54–55, **64**,
               83–84, 102
   Liability for damages.... **20**, 67
   Naturalization certificate,
      copying or notarizing..... 65
   Overcharging **65**, 87
   Personal appearance,
      failure to require .. **65**, 82, 89

Preparing document.... 16–17,
                  54–55
Professional license,
   action on other ... **64**, 76–77
Qualifications, failure to
   maintain **63–64**, 103
Revocation **63**, 76–77, 82
Seal/Stamp,
   disposition of **66**, 101
   unauthorized
      manufacturing.. **66**, 77, 100
   exclusive property.. **66**, 78–79
Serious crime defined. ... **62**, 75
Signature, notarizing own .. **64**,
                  77–78
Signature, obtaining
   under duress........ **65**, 87
Testimonials **65**, 103
Stamp/Seal
   disposition of **66**, 101
   unauthorized
      manufacturing.. **66**, 77, 100
   exclusive property.. **66**, 78–79

N

Name, change of **21–22**, 101
National Notary
   Association 114
Naturalization certificates .. 60, 65
Notarial acts **22–38**, 75
   Acknowledgment ... 22, **23–28**,
                  77–78,
               79–80, 97
   Affidavit.............. 30–31
   Affirmation **32–34**, 75
   Authorized acts **22–23**, 75
   Certified copies 11, 22,
                 28–29,
              77–78, 80
   Choosing............ 15–16,
                  16–17,
                46, 102
   Deposition 22, **29–30**, 85
   Jurat 22, **30–31**, 75,
                77–78, 79–80

INDEX

Oath 22, **32–34**, 75
Proof of acknowledgment
 by subscribing witness . . . 23,
  34–35
Proof of execution (see
 Proof of acknowledgment. . 23,
  34–35
Protest 23, **36–38**,
  90–95
Unauthorized acts 23
Verification upon oath
 or affirmation 22, **30–31**,
  75, *77–78*,
  79–80
Notarial certificates (see
 Certificates, notarial) 7,
  15–16, 25–26,
  29, 31, 32, 35,
  36, 37–38, **43–48**,
  79–80, 97
Notarial records (see Journal
 of notarial acts) 6–7,
  15, **41–43**
Notary seal (see Seal/Stamp,
 Notary) 4–5, 16,
  49–51, 77,
  78–79, 100–101

O

Oath 22, **32–34**, 75
 Ceremony. 33–34
 Corporate. 32–33
 Credible identifying
  witnesses, for 33, **40**
 Deposition, for. 30
 Fees 52, *100–101*
 Gestures. 33–34
 Jurat, for 31
 Power to administer. . . . **32**, 75
 Purpose 32
 Response required 33

Verification, for **31**, 75
 Wording 33
Oath of office, Notary's . . .4, **20**,
  75–76

P

Penalties (see
 Misconduct) **62–67**, 75,
  *76–77, 82, 83–84,
  86–87, 89–90, 103*
Personal appearance **13**, 65,
  82, 89
Personal knowledge of
 identity **39**, *77–78*
Photocopies 10
Photographs, notarizing 9
Practices and procedures . .38–62
Proof of acknowledgment
 by subscribing witness . .23, **35**
Protest 23,
  36–38, *90–95*
 Antiquated act 37
 Certificate. **37–38**, *94–95*
 Fees **52**, *100–101*
 Purpose 36–37
 Special knowledge
  required 37
Prothonotary, certificate of
 (see Authentication) 57–58
Proxy, signing by (see Disabled
 signer, signing for) **55–56**,
  77–78, 98

Q

Qualifications . .3, **18–19**, *75–76*

R

Reasonable care 13–17,
  53–54

Page numbers listed in **bold** indicate where the most complete information on a subject can be found. *Italics* indicate the pages where the statutes pertaining to a subject are located.

121

Records (see Journal of
  notarial acts) 6–7,
  15, **41–43**
Refusal of services 53
Resignation **21**, *82, 103*
Restricting services 10
Revised Code of Washington
  (RCW) (see Washington,
  Revised Code of) *74–99*
Revocation (see
  Misconduct) **63**, *76–77, 82*

S

Satisfactory evidence 24, 27,
  42, *77–78,*
  96, 103
Scilicet 43
SCT. 43
Seal/Stamp, Notary 4–5,
  16, **49–51**, 77,
  78–79, 100–101
Affixing 16, **49**, *78–79*
Disposition of. **50–51**, *101*
Embosser 50
Format. **49–50**, *100*
Information required. **49**,
  77, *100*
Lost or stolen. **50**, *100*
L.S. **44**, 50
Manufacturing,
  unlawful. **50**, *102*
No room for. 9–10
Placement of 50
Requirement **49**, 77, *100*
Sharing **51**, *78–79*
Smearing 9–10
Secretary of State's
  office 3, **105**
Self-notarization . . .23, **64**, *77–78*
Signature, Notary's
  Certificate, on 44
  Checking 14
  In presence of Notary . . . 11–12
  Journal 42
  Minor, of. 57

Mark, signature by 55
Notarizing one's own. . . 23, **64**,
  77–78
Notary's. 16, 44
Witnessing or attesting. 22,
  31–32,
  77–78, 79–80
Signature by mark 55
  Certificate for. 55
  Procedures 55
  Witnesses 55
SS. .43
Stamp/Seal, Notary (see
  Seal/Stamp, Notary) 4–5,
  16, **49–51**, 77,
  78–79, 100–101
Statement of particulars
  (see Certificate) 44
Statutes pertaining to
  notarization *74–104*
Subscribing witness
  (see Proof of
  acknowledgment
  by subscribing witness) . .23, **35**
Supplies 6–7
Surety **20**, *76*

T

Telephone notarizations . .13, **23**,
  24, 30
Term of office **20–21**, 77
Testimonium clause
  (see Certificate) 44
Thumbprint, journal 7
  Device 7
Tools, Notary 6–7

U

U.S. Code:
  10 U.S.C. Sec. 936 61
  10 U.S.C. Sec. 1044a. 61
  18 U.S.C. Sec. 137. . . . . . 60, 65
U.S. Penal Code:
  Section 75 . . . . 60, 65

INDEX

V

Venue (see Certificate) 43
   Stamp. 7
Verification upon oath
   or affirmation 22, **30–31**,
                              75, 77–78,
                              79–80
   Affirmation for. 31
   Certificate **31**, 79–80
   Identification **31**, 77–78
   Jurat. 30, 75, 77–78
   Oath for 31
   Purpose **30–31**, 77–78
Vital records, notarizing . . .11, **29**
Vital Statistics,
   Bureaus of 106–110

W

Washington Administrative
Code (WAC):
   308-30-005 . . . . *100*
   308-30-010. . . . . 22, 49,
                          50, 66, *100*
   308-30-020. . . . . 51, 52,
                        65, *100–101*
   308-30-030 . . . . *101*
   308-30-040 . . . . 21, 51, 66, *101*
   308-30-050. . . . . 50, *101*
   308-30-060 . . . . 21, 22, *101*
   308-30-070. . . . . 57, 58,
                            101–102
   308-30-080. . . . . 67, *102*
   308-30-090. . . . . 46, 55,
                        60, 64, *102*
   308-30-100. . . . . 19, 22,
                              50, *102*
   308-30-120. . . . . 43, *102*
   308-30-130. . . . . 49, *102*
   308-30-140. . . . . 64, *103*
   308-30-150 . . . . 21, 64, *103*
   308-30-155. . . . . 38, 39,
                          40, 41, *103*
   308-30-160. . . . . 23, 36,
                             65, *103*
   308-30-170 . . . . *103*
   308-30-180. . . . . *103–104*
   308-30-190 . . . . *104*
Washington, Revised
Code of (RCW):
   2.48.170. . . . . 55, 64, *83*
   2.48.180 . . . . 55, 64, *83–84*
   5.28.010 . . . . 30, *85*
   5.28.020 . . . . 30, *85*
   5.28.030 . . . . *85*
   5.28.040 . . . . 30, *85*
   5.28.050 . . . . *85*
   5.28.060 . . . . *85*
   5.52.050 . . . . 48, *86*
   9A.60.010 . . . . *86*
   9A.60.020. . . . . 48, 65, *87*
   9A.60.030 . . . . 65, *87*
   9A.60.040 . . . . *87*
   9A.60.050 . . . . *87*
   9A.68.020. . . . . 52, 65, *87*
   9A.80.010. . . . . 66, *87–88*
   26.04.150. . . . . 57, *88*
   36.18.010 . . . . *88*
   42.20.020. . . . . 66, *89*
   42.20.030 . . . . *89*
   42.20.040 . . . . *89*
   42.20.050 . . . . 48, 65, *89*
   42.20.100 . . . . 53, *89–90*
   42.44.010 . . . . 22, 24, 25,
                        28, 30, 32,
                        39, 62, 75
   42.44.020. . . . . 18, 20,
                          21, 75–76
   42.44.030 . . . . 18, 19, 62,
                      63, 64, 76–77
   42.44.040 77
   42.44.050 . . . . 49, 66, 77
   42.44.060 . . . . 20, 21, 77
   42.44.070. . . . . 19, 77
   42.44.080 . . . . . . 22, 23, 24, 27,
                   29, 30, 31, 35,
                   38, 39, 40, 41,
               53, 56, 64, 77–78
   42.44.090 . . . . 43, 49, 51,
                    54, 66, 78–79
   42.44.100 . . . . . . 25, 26, 29, 31,
                 32, 36, 46, 79–80

42.44.110. . . . . 48, *80*
42.44.120. . . . . 52, *80*
42.44.130 . . . . . . 27, 28, *80–81*
42.44.140 . . . . *81*
42.44.150. . . . . *81–82*
42.44.160. . . . . 48, 62,
                        64, 65, *82*
42.44.170 . . . . 21, 63, *82*
42.44.180 . . . . 57, 58, *82*
42.44.190 . . . . *82*
42.44.200. . . . . *82–83*
42.44.900 . . . . *83*
42.44.901 . . . . *83*
42.44.902 . . . . *83*
42.44.903 . . . . *83*
62A.3-501 . . . . 37, *90*
62A.3-502. . . . . 37, *90–92*
62A.3-503 . . . . 37, *92*
62A.3-504 . . . . *92–93*
62A.3-505 . . . . 37, *93*
62A.3-512 . . . . *93*
62A.3-515 . . . . *93–94*
62A.3-520. . . . . 37, *94–95*
62A.3-522. . . . . 37, 38, *95*
62A.3-525 . . . . *95*
64.08.010 . . . . 27, *95–96*
64.08.020. . . . . 27, *96*
64.08.040. . . . . 28, *96*
64.08.050. . . . . *96–97*
64.08.060. . . . . 25, *97*
64.08.070. . . . . 25, *97*
64.08.090. . . . . 27, *98*
64.08.100. . . . . 56, *98*
65.04.045 . . . . 45, *98–99*
Weddings (see Marriages) 23
Willingness,
  determining 13–14
Wills 8–9, **61–62**
  Advice or assistance 61
  Certificate required. 62
  Living wills 62
Witnessing or attesting
  signature 22, **31–32**,
                       77–78, 79–80
  Certificate **32**, 79–80
  Purpose **31–32**, 77–78

Because you can't know everything...

You Should Belong to the National Notary Association

It doesn't matter whether you're a long-time Notary, or a newcomer. Whether you notarize dozens of documents each week, or a few a month.

As a Notary, you should belong to the National Notary Association.

We're a professional association with over 150,000 members from every state and U.S. jurisdiction. And we've devoted our efforts to your needs and concerns for over four decades.

There are many reasons to be a part of the NNA. Among them:

- *The National Notary* magazine... A bimonthly magazine packed with enlightening articles, helpful how-to features, handy tips and useful advice.

- The *Notary Bulletin* newspaper... This bimonthly newspaper keeps you up-to-date on law and procedure changes in your state, and helps you comply with new laws.

- Discount Notary Supplies... You'll save up to 40% on the supplies you need, including Notary journals, official seals, certificates and more.

With these services and so much more, we're here for you when you need us. You should belong to the National Notary Association.

National Notary Association
9350 De Soto Ave., P.O. Box 2402
Chatsworth, CA 91313-2402
Telephone: 1-800-US NOTARY (1-800-876-6827)
Fax: 1-800-833-1211
www.nationalnotary.org

Other Resources from the National Notary Association

'Notary Law & Practice: Cases & Materials'
...The definitive legal text on notarization. Authored by five noted law school professors, *Notary Law & Practice* presents scores of notarization-related court decisions and details how these cases affect you today. You get extensive judicial opinions and commentary about notarizations and related frauds. Hardcover, 6¼" x 9¼", 629 pages.

No. 5100............................$49.95 NNA members / $68.00 non-NNA members

'Notary Home Study Course'
...Step-by-step, illustrated instructions for all the notarial acts you'll likely perform. You'll learn how to complete the many certificates you'll see, notarize unusual documents, avoid common pitfalls, and prevent personal liability. Learn time-saving shortcuts you can take...and can't take. The *Notary Home Study Course* will make your duties as a Notary much, much easier! Softcover, 8¼" x 10¾", 448 pages.

No. 5001............................$34.95 NNA members / $48.00 non-NNA members

'Notary Seal & Certificate Verification Manual'
...Essential for legal and business professionals and government officials who receive or send documents out-of-state. At a glance, the *Notary Seal & Certificate Verification Manual* gives you detailed notarization rules and procedures for all 50 states, the District of Columbia, and five U.S. jurisdictions. Softcover, 8¼" x 10¾", 423 pages.

No. 5143............................$44.95 NNA members / $79.00 non-NNA members

'Notary Basics Made Easy' Video Instruction Program
...Makes reviewing Notary basics as easy as watching TV. From checking signer's identification to affixing your signature and seal, *Notary Basics Made Easy* gives you the know-how you need to begin or enhance your career as a Notary. Complete set includes three VHS video tapes and a handy 16-page Program Guide. Approximate running time: 50 minutes.

No. 5009............................$29.95 NNA members / $50.00 non-NNA members

'State Notary Law Primers'
...Detailed instructions on Notary laws and regulations in the following states:

Arizona ....No. 5130	Missouri ....No. 5122	Oregon ....No. 5128
California........No. 5120	Nevada ....No. 5134	Texas ....No. 5123
Florida ....No. 5121	New Jersey ......No. 5131	Utah..............No. 5127
Hawaii............No. 5132	New York ....No. 5125	Washington ....No. 5124
Michigan ....No. 5135	No. Carolina ....No. 5129	*(More states in production.)*

Softcover, 124 to 128 pages, 5¼" x 8⅜"......$12.95 NNA members / $16.00 non-NNA members

---

National Notary Association
To order, use the form on the back of the opposite page, or call 1-800-876-6827.

'101 Useful Notary Tips'
...Tips on every subject, from acknowledgments and apostilles...to jurats and journals...to seals and signatures make this a perfect, quick reference guide. Softcover, 5½" x 8¼", 46 pages.

No. 5119 .... $8.95 NNA members / $14.00 non-NNA members

'12 Steps to a Flawless Notarization'
...Explains how to perform a problem-free notarization, including screening identification, scanning a document and filling out notarial wording. Softcover, 5¼" x 8¼", 48 pages.

No. 5144 .... $8.95 NNA members / $14.00 non-NNA members

'ID Checking Guide'
...Pictures and specifications for each state's driver's license, descriptions of non-driver, military and immigration IDs, and credit cards. Drivers License Guide Co., softcover, 6" x 9", 96 pages.

No. 5599.......................... $17.95 NNA members / $20.00 non-NNA members

'How to Fingerprint'
...Shows you all the steps for taking clear, useable fingerprints for employment, for a special office or for identification of minors. Softcover, 5¼" x 8¼", 110 pages.

No. 5102.......................... $12.95 NNA members / $18.00 non-NNA members

'How to Take a Notary Journal Thumbprint'
...Explains how a journal thumbprint protects the Notary, document signers and the public. Provides details on how to obtain clear, useable prints. Softcover, 5¼" x 8¼", 64 pages.

No. 5140 .... $8.95 NNA members / $14.00 non-NNA members

'Notary Public Practices & Glossary'
...Covers every important facet of the Notary Public office and provides definitive explanations of notarial procedures. Hardcover, 5½" x 8¾", 176 pages.

No. 5110.......................... $15.95 NNA members / $22.00 non-NNA members

'Preparing for the California Notary Public Exam'
...Helps you get ready for and pass the exam by explaining California's stringent Notary laws and focusing on what is important for the exam. Softcover, 5¼" x 8¼", 88 pages.

No. 2000.......................... $12.95 NNA members / $18.00 non-NNA members

'Sorry, No Can Do!' & 'Sorry, No Can Do! 2'
...Easy-to-understand responses to the most common requests for improper notarizations. When asked to preform an improper act, you can show your signer the relevant page and they'll see why you have to turn down the request. Hardcover, 5¼" x 8¼", spiral bound to lay flat.

2 Volume Set, No. 5386 .... $21.95 NNA members / $30.00 non-NNA members

---

National Notary Association
To order, use the form on the back of this page, or call 1-800-876-6827.

Order Form

Membership Information

☐ **YES!** I want to receive the benefits of membership in the National Notary Association! Please enroll me as a member for the following term:

☐ 1 Year $34
☐ 2 Years $59 – save $9.00!
☐ 3 Years $79 – save $23.00!
☐ 4 Years $99 – save $37.00!
☐ 5 Years – $119 save $51.00!

Please include your membership dues in total below. There is no tax or shipping charge on your NNA membership.

Item #	Quantity	Description	Price	TOTAL

SHIPPING

Subtotal	Shipping
UNDER $15	$3.85
$15.01 – $35.00	$4.85
$35.01 – $65.00	$5.85
$65.01 – $95.00	$6.85
$95.01+	$7.85

Subtotal _____
Add state and local taxes on subtotal for: AZ, CA, FL, MI, MO, NV, NJ, NY, TX & WA _____
Add Shipping _____
Add Membership Dues _____
TOTAL Enclosed _____

Shipping/Payment Information

Name _____
Organization _____
Address ☐ Business ☐ Home _____
City _____
State _____ Zip _____
Daytime Phone _____
Fax _____
E-Mail Address _____

NNA Member Number (Required for member prices) _____

☐ Check Enclosed — Payable to: National Notary Association

☐ Visa ☐ MasterCard ☐ American Express ☐ Discover

Card Number _____
Card Expires _____
Signature _____

Sorry, but we cannot accept purchase orders to bill on account.

Four Easy Ways to Order:

By Phone: 1-800-876-6827
(1-800-US NOTARY) with credit card order

By FAX: 1-800-833-1211
24 hours with credit card order

By Mail: NNA Notary Supplies Division
9350 De Soto Ave., P.O. Box 2402
Chatsworth, CA 91313-2402

By Internet: www.nationalnotary.org
24 hours with credit card order

National Notary Association

Office use only.

Service Code
A15745